Celebrating Sunday for Catholic Families
2022–2023

Kerri Mecke-Lozano

LTP
LITURGY
TRAINING
PUBLICATIONS

Nihil Obstat   Imprimatur
Rev. Mr. Daniel G. Welter, JD   Most Rev. Robert G. Casey
Chancellor   Vicar General
Archdiocese of Chicago   Archdiocese of Chicago
September 8, 2021   September 8, 2021

The *Nihil Obstat* and *Imprimatur* are declarations that the material is free from doctrinal or moral error, and thus is granted permission to publish in accordance with c. 827. No legal responsibility is assumed by the grant of this permission. No implication is contained herein that those who have granted the *Nihil Obstat* and *Imprimatur* agree with the content, opinions, or statements expressed.

CELEBRATING SUNDAY FOR CATHOLIC FAMILIES 2022–2023 © 2022 Archdiocese of Chicago: Liturgy Training Publications, 3949 South Racine Avenue, Chicago, IL 60609; 800-933-1800; fax: 800-933-7094; email: orders@ltp.org; website: www.LTP.org. All rights reserved.

This book was edited by Michaela I. Tudela. Víctor R. Pérez was the production editor, Anna Manhart was the designer, and Kari Nicholls was the production artist.

Cover art © William Hernandez.

Printed in the United States of America

ISBN: 978-1-61671-653-0

CSCF23

"You shall love the Lord your God with all your heart, and with all your soul, and with all your might. Keep these words that I am commanding to you today in your heart. Recite them to your children and talk about them when you are at home and when you are away, when you lie down and when you rise."

(Deuteronomy 6:5–7)

Contents

How to Use
Celebrating Sunday
for Catholic Families

This small weekly guide draws on the Gospel for each
Sunday and holy day for the coming year. It is intended to
help parents engage their children with the Mass and deepen
their appreciation of the richness of their faith life. So often,
going to Mass becomes a weekly event that begins and ends at
the church door. The brief reflection on an excerpt from the
Gospel is intended to spark your thinking about the Scripture
that will lead to conversation with your family before and
after Mass. Suggestions for questions and conversation starters
are provided, as well as some practice or practical way to
carry this reflection into the life of the family. Keep in mind,
however, that sometimes you may have other needs, concerns,
or ideas that are more relevant to your home life at that
moment. If so, engage your children with those.

Note that very young children are able to enter into the
liturgy through their senses. Singing the hymns, calling their
attention to the changing colors of the liturgical seasons, and
sitting where they can observe the gestures of the Mass are
all ways to form them in the faith. Always remember, as the
Rite of Baptism proclaims, you, as parents, are your children's
first and most important teachers. We hope that this book
will enrich your family's life of faith.

September 4, 2022

Twenty-Third Sunday in Ordinary Time

Hearing the Word

Luke 14:25–33

In the name of the Father, and of the Son, and of the Holy Spirit.

Great crowds were traveling with Jesus, and he turned and addressed them, "If anyone comes to me without hating his father and mother, wife and children, brothers and sisters, and even his own life, he cannot be my disciple. Whoever does not carry his own cross and come after me cannot be my disciple. Which of you wishing to construct a tower does not first sit down and calculate the cost to see if there is enough for its completion? Otherwise, after laying the foundation and finding himself unable to finish the work the onlookers should laugh at him and say, 'This one began to build but did not have the resources to finish.' Or what king marching into battle would not first sit down and decide whether with ten thousand troops he can successfully oppose another king advancing upon him with twenty thousand troops? But if not, while he is still far away, he will send a delegation to ask for peace terms. In the same way, anyone of you who does not renounce all his possessions cannot be my disciple."

Reflecting on the Word

At first glance this Scripture passage seems, well, wrong! Jesus wants us to hate our mother and father? If we go back and look at the original language, however, we see that the word *hate* here is an expression that is better translated as "preference." Jesus is telling us that we should not prefer anyone, even our family, or anything in our lives before him, or we cannot be his disciple. He defines for us what a disciple is: someone who puts Jesus before everyone and everything. Jesus doesn't want us to abandon our families or to hate them. That wouldn't follow his teachings on loving and respecting our parents. If we prioritize him, then our lives will have the proper foundation.

......ON THE WAY TO MASS

What does it mean to be a disciple of Jesus Christ?

ON THE WAY HOME FROM MASS ......

What are some ways that we could make Jesus first in our lives?

Living the Word

Throughout this week find ways to make Jesus more important in your family's life. Before you get out of bed in the morning, talk to him. Before you eat or play a game, thank him for what's in front of you. When you are nervous or afraid, remember Jesus is there and thank him for being with you. As you drive in your car, talk or think about one moment from Jesus' life.

Twenty-Fourth Sunday in Ordinary Time

Hearing the Word

Luke 15:1–7

In the name of the Father, and of the Son, and of the Holy Spirit.

Tax collectors and sinners were all drawing near to listen to Jesus, but the Pharisees and scribes began to complain, saying, "This man welcomes sinners and eats with them." So to them he addressed this parable. "What man among you having a hundred sheep and losing one of them would not leave the ninety-nine in the desert and go after the lost one until he finds it? And when he does find it, he sets it on his shoulders with great joy and, upon his arrival home, he calls together his friends and neighbors and says to them, 'Rejoice with me because I have found my lost sheep.' I tell you, in just the same way there will be more joy in heaven over one sinner who repents than over ninety-nine righteous people who have no need of repentance."

Reflecting on the Word

I wonder how the sheep felt when he was lost. The shepherd didn't wait for his sheep to return. He proactively sought it out. He would have never stopped looking. When that lost sheep saw the Good Shepherd and was placed on his shoulders, he must have felt such relief, such gratefulness, and so loved. Jesus' heart was so joyful he even wants to celebrate! We sometimes stray from Jesus, make choices that separate us from him. He has such love for us, however, that he will never stop seeking us out. When we have returned to his side through the sacrament of reconciliation, he has such joy!

•••••• ON THE WAY TO MASS

When have you been lost or felt alone? How did it feel when you were found?

ON THE WAY HOME FROM MASS ••••••

We just celebrated with Jesus at Mass. What are some other ways that we celebrate being with Jesus?

Living the Word

As a family this week, celebrate the sacrament of reconciliation at your parish. Bring the whole family, even if some are too young to celebrate. As a family, discuss how it feels before and after celebrating this merciful sacrament. Ponder if it might be how the sheep felt when he was lost and then found.

September 18, 2022

Twenty-Fifth Sunday in Ordinary Time

Hearing the Word

Luke 16:10–13

In the name of the Father, and of the Son, and of the Holy Spirit.

Jesus said to his disciples, "The person who is trustworthy in very small matters is also trustworthy in great ones; and the person who is dishonest in very small matters is also dishonest in great ones. If, therefore, you are not trustworthy with dishonest wealth, who will trust you with true wealth? If you are not trustworthy with what belongs to another, who will give you what is yours? No servant can serve two masters. He will either hate one and love the other, or be devoted to one and despise the other. You cannot serve both God and mammon."

Reflecting on the Word

What does it mean to be trustworthy? If we are willing to lie about the small matters: the broken dish, the unbrushed teeth, the bad decision, then it makes it easier to lie about the big stuff in life. But what if Jesus is also speaking about being trustworthy with opportunities to bring his love into the world. Most of us won't save the world in big ways; most of us will save it by the small acts of love that we can do every day of our lives. If Jesus can trust us with our present time in this world, then he will entrust us with the great kingdom of heaven.

• • • • • • ON THE WAY TO MASS

What does it mean to be trustworthy?

ON THE WAY HOME FROM MASS • • • • • •

How can we be faithful to and worthy of trust in the small opportunities to love in our everyday lives?

Living the Word

Throughout the week look for opportunities to praise your family members for being honest. Notice the small things that they are being honest about and thank them for their honesty. Also look for the small acts of love that you can do or that you see others do. You are spreading God's love!

September 25, 2022

Twenty-Sixth Sunday in Ordinary Time

Hearing the Word

Luke 16:19–25

In the name of the Father, and of the Son, and of the Holy Spirit.

Jesus said to the Pharisees, "There was a rich man who dressed in purple garments and fine linen and dined sumptuously each day. And lying at his door was a poor man named Lazarus, covered with sores, who would gladly have eaten his fill of the scraps that fell from the rich man's table. Dogs even used to come and lick his sores. When the poor man died, he was carried away by angels to the bosom of Abraham. The rich man also died and was buried, and from the netherworld, where he was in torment, he raised his eyes and saw Abraham far off and Lazarus at his side. And he cried out, 'Father Abraham, have pity on me. Send Lazarus to dip the tip of his finger in water and cool my tongue, for I am suffering torment in these flames.' Abraham replied, 'My child, remember that you received what was good during your lifetime while Lazarus likewise received what was bad; but now he is comforted here, whereas you are tormented.'"

Reflecting on the Word

In Jewish culture, a name is very important. A name gives purpose and meaning. Jesus conveys who is important in the parable of a poor man named Lazarus and a rich man who is unnamed. The rich man has every physical thing he needs but no meaning or purpose to his life. A very poor man lives at his doorstep, but the rich man doesn't seem to concern himself with him. The rich man has chosen to live his life for himself, not for God, not for others. We can choose better. Jesus is our example of how to love and how to live our lives for God.

· · · · · · ON THE WAY TO MASS

Is there anything in our lives (items, habits, and so on) that is keeping us from living our lives for Jesus and others?

ON THE WAY HOME FROM MASS · · · · · ·

How can we better follow Jesus' example to love those around us who need our love and attention?

Living the Word

Who do you know might be lonely? Call, visit, or write a letter to that person. Let them know that you were thinking of them and let them share how they are doing. Pray for this person throughout your week.

October 2, 2022

Twenty-Seventh Sunday in Ordinary Time

Hearing the Word

Luke 17:5–10

In the name of the Father, and of the Son, and of the Holy Spirit.

The apostles said to the Lord, "Increase our faith." The Lord replied, "If you have faith the size of a mustard seed, you would say to this mulberry tree, 'Be uprooted and planted in the sea,' and it would obey you.

"Who among you would say to your servant who has just come in from plowing or tending sheep in the field, 'Come here immediately and take your place at table'? Would he not rather say to him, 'Prepare something for me to eat. Put on your apron and wait on me while I eat and drink. You may eat and drink when I am finished'? Is he grateful to that servant because he did what was commanded? So should it be with you. When you have done all you have been commanded, say, 'We are unprofitable servants; we have done what we were obliged to do."

Reflecting on the Word

Jesus' apostles who saw him work miracles were asking for their faith to increase. They knew faith is a gift from God. They knew they must ask for it. When God gives us the gift of faith and we use it, we can do mighty things. When great works come from our mustard seed–sized faith, we must humble ourselves and remember where the faith came from. It is not by our doing but by God's.

...... ON THE WAY TO MASS

What does it mean to be humble? How can we be more humble before God, who gives us everything we have?

ON THE WAY HOME FROM MASS ......

Would you like to ask Jesus to increase your faith? What might God do with your increased faith?

Living the Word

Throughout the week ask God to increase your faith. Notice all the gifts he gives you every day and humble yourself before him in thanksgiving.

Twenty-Eighth Sunday in Ordinary Time

Hearing the Word

Luke 17:11–19

In the name of the Father, and of the Son, and of the Holy Spirit.

As Jesus continued his journey to Jerusalem, he traveled through Samaria and Galilee. As he was entering a village, ten lepers met him. They stood at a distance from him and raised their voice saying, "Jesus, Master! Have pity on us!" And when he saw them, he said, "Go show yourselves to the priests." As they were going they were cleansed. And one of them, realizing he had been healed, returned, glorifying God in a loud voice; and he fell at the feet of Jesus and thanked him. He was a Samaritan. Jesus said in reply, "Ten were cleansed, were they not? Where are the other nine? Has none but this foreigner returned to give thanks to God?" Then he said to him, "Stand up and go; your faith has saved you."

Reflecting on the Word

Am I like the nine lepers, who when cured joyfully ran back to their life, or am I like the one, who when cured remembered the source of that gift and went back to give thanks? Some days I am like the nine: I go through my day too busy or distracted to notice the gifts, big and small, that surround me. Some days I am like the one, pausing to remember and thank God for everything, and I mean everything! It is on these days that I have more joy. It is gratitude that opens my eyes to even more gifts that have already been given by the one who loves me most. God does not need us to thank him, but he knows that being thankful brings us joy and closer to him. Everything is a gift.

......ON THE WAY TO MASS

What are gifts that God gives us every day that we don't often stop and thank him for?

ON THE WAY HOME FROM MASS ......

On days where we are busy or unhappy, how can we remind ourselves of the gifts that God has given us that day?

Living the Word

As a family, play the "Thank You, God" game. Take turns telling God something you are grateful for. For example, "Thank you, God, for the pretty flowers." "Thank you, God, for the working refrigerator." "Thank you, God, for my family." See how long your list of things to be grateful for grows!

Twenty-Ninth Sunday in Ordinary Time

Hearing the Word

Luke 18:1-8

In the name of the Father, and of the Son, and of the Holy Spirit.

Jesus told his disciples a parable about the necessity for them to pray always without becoming weary. He said, "There was a judge in a certain town who neither feared God nor respected any human being. And a widow in that town used to come to him and say, 'Render a just decision for me against my adversary.' For a long time the judge was unwilling, but eventually he thought, 'While it is true that I neither fear God nor respect any human being, because this widow keeps bothering me I shall deliver a just decision for her lest she finally come and strike me.'" The Lord said, "Pay attention to what the dishonest judge says. Will not God then secure the rights of his chosen ones who call out to him day and night? Will he be slow to answer them? I tell you, he will see to it that justice is done for them speedily. But when the Son of Man comes, will he find faith on earth?"

Reflecting on the Word

Does our persistence in prayer change God's response? Or does the praying "always without becoming weary" change our own hearts? God's love for us is without end. It doesn't waver when times are hard. What about our faith? Will God find faith when he gazes on us? The widow in the parable, although her life is difficult, doesn't give up faith that she will be heard. She is a beautiful example for us to pray always. Pray as though we know God is listening. Pray inviting God in the small, everyday moments of life and into the big moments. If the unjust judge would listen and answer the widow, how much more would our God listen and answer our prayers?

• • • • • • ON THE WAY TO MASS

When do we pray? When can we try and pray more often during our day?

ON THE WAY HOME FROM MASS • • • • • •

What do we pray about? Sometimes it is easier to pray when we need something, but what else can we talk to God about? Do we listen to God responding to us as well?

Living the Word

This week, gather a few times as a family and pray together at home. It doesn't have to take very long, take five to ten minutes to sing a hymn together, take turns praying, or read Scripture aloud. It's all right if prayer becomes unstructured and loud. Don't get discouraged if it is not perfect, keep trying. At the end of the week, talk together about the experience.

October 23, 2022

THIRTIETH SUNDAY IN ORDINARY TIME

Hearing the Word

Luke 18:9–14

In the name of the Father, and of the Son, and of the Holy Spirit.

Jesus addressed this parable to those who were convinced of their own righteousness and despised everyone else. "Two people went up to the temple area to pray; one was a Pharisee and the other was a tax collector. The Pharisee took up his position and spoke this prayer to himself, 'O God, I thank you that I am not like the rest of humanity—greedy, dishonest, adulterous—or even like this tax collector. I fast twice a week, and I pay tithes on my whole income.' But the tax collector stood off at a distance and would not even raise his eyes to heaven but beat his breast and prayed, 'O God, be merciful to me a sinner.' I tell you, the latter went home justified, not the former; for whoever exalts himself will be humbled, and the one who humbles himself will be exalted."

Reflecting on the Word

In Jesus' time, Pharisees followed the Jewish law strictly and spent a lot of time in the temple praying. Tax collectors of the day were despised because they took more tax money than needed from people and pocketed the excess. So why does Jesus criticize the Pharisee and praise the tax collector? The Pharisee, in lifting up all his good deeds, compared himself to others, thinking himself superior. He feels he has earned his position before God. His prayer is to himself, praising himself. The tax collector, knowing his own faults, prays to God asking for his mercy. His focus is on God, knowing he is in desperate need of his mercy. Our worth does not come from our good or bad deeds; it comes from being a child of God. Nothing can change our value in God's eyes. We must respect each other, not because the person has done good things but because they are a beloved child of God.

......ON THE WAY TO MASS

When you pray, do you think more about God in all his goodness or about yourself?

ON THE WAY HOME FROM MASS ......

Have you ever humbly asked God for forgiveness like the tax collector? What do you think was God's response?

Living the Word

This week research images of the parable of the Pharisee and the tax collector. Discuss how each are portrayed. Do the colors, textures, and scenes align with what Jesus was teaching?

October 30, 2022

Thirty-First Sunday in Ordinary Time

Hearing the Word

Luke 19:1–10

In the name of the Father, and of the Son, and of the Holy Spirit.

Jesus came to Jericho and intended to pass through the town. Now a man there named Zacchaeus, who was a chief tax collector and also a wealthy man, was seeking to see who Jesus was; but he could not see him because of the crowd, for he was short in stature. So he ran ahead and climbed a sycamore tree in order to see Jesus, who was about to pass that way. When he reached the place, Jesus looked up and said to him, "Zacchaeus, come down quickly, for today I must stay at your house." And he came down quickly and received him with joy. When they all saw this, they began to grumble, saying, "He has gone to stay at the house of a sinner." But Zacchaeus stood there and said to the Lord, "Behold, half of my possessions, Lord, I shall give to the poor, and if I have extorted anything from anyone I shall repay it four times over." And Jesus said to him, "Today salvation has come to this house because this man too is a descendant of Abraham. For the Son of Man has come to seek and to save what was lost."

Reflecting on the Word

How badly do we want to encounter Jesus? Zacchaeus, who was not well liked in his community, was willing to risk looking foolish and climb a tree just to get a glimpse. That desire in his heart to encounter him was not missed by Jesus. Jesus saw both Zacchaeus' sinfulness and the longings of his heart. So he did something very intimate: He called him by his name. When someone doesn't know your name, you feel invisible. Jesus noticed Zacchaeus—and he knows us. He sees both our sinfulness and our goodness. With that full, complete picture of who we are, he calls us by name and desires to stay with us.

...... ON THE WAY TO MASS

How much do you risk sometimes to encounter Jesus?

ON THE WAY HOME FROM MASS ......

How would it feel for Jesus to call out your name and ask to stay in your house?

Living the Word

Talk together about how each person got their name. Where did it come from, what does it mean? Also, look up the many names for Jesus. Which one is your favorite? Use different names for God or Jesus in your prayer time together.

Solemnity of All Saints

Hearing the Word
Matthew 5:3–12a

In the name of the Father, and of the Son, and of the Holy Spirit.

[Jesus said]: "Blessed are the poor in spirit, / for theirs is the Kingdom of heaven. / Blessed are they who mourn, / for they will be comforted. / Blessed are the meek, / for they will inherit the land. / Blessed are they who hunger and thirst for righteousness, / for they will be satisfied. / Blessed are the merciful, / for they will be shown mercy. / Blessed are the clean of heart, / for they will see Gód. / Blessed are the peace-makers, / for they will be called children of God. / Blessed are they who are persecuted for the sake of righteousness, / for theirs is the Kingdom of heaven. / Blessed are you when they insult you and persecute you / and utter every kind of evil against you [falsely] because of me. / Rejoice and be glad, / for your reward will be great in heaven."

Reflecting on the Word

The world around us has many ideas on how we should live our lives and how it measures success. In the Beatitudes, Jesus is showing us the way to sainthood. His definition of success is not good grades, money, popularity, or good looks, but humility, showing mercy and forgiveness, and seeking truth. These characteristics are very different from one another. The Bible reminds us, however, that God's ways are not like our ways, but that they will give us complete joy. The saints are powerful examples to us of human beings who are imperfect but who have tried to live out these Beatitudes and now have their reward in heaven. May we have the strength and desire to follow their examples.

• • • • • • ON THE WAY TO MASS

The word *Beatitude* means "blessedness," or "happiness." Who in your life is blessed? Why?

ON THE WAY HOME FROM MASS • • • • • •

How do the Beatitudes make you feel? Which one is your favorite?

Living the Word

Choose one Beatitude to discuss together. Ponder its meaning throughout the week. Your family might also write a few new Beatitudes.

Thirty-Second Sunday in Ordinary Time

Hearing the Word

Luke 20:27, 34–38

In the name of the Father, and of the Son, and of the Holy Spirit.

Some Sadducees, those who deny that there is a resurrection, came forward.

Jesus said to them, "The children of this age marry and remarry; but those who are deemed worthy to attain to the coming age and to the resurrection of the dead neither marry nor are given in marriage. They can no longer die, for they are like angels; and they are the children of God because they are the ones who will rise. That the dead will rise even Moses made known in the passage about the bush, when he called 'Lord,' the God of Abraham, the God of Isaac, and the God of Jacob; and he is not God of the dead, but of the living, for to him all are alive."

Reflecting on the Word

The Sadducees were questioning Jesus because what Jesus taught about the resurrection and life after death was not what they believed. So, what was Jesus teaching about life after death? When Jesus died and then rose from the dead he did not just come back to life, he was transformed! His own friends did not recognize him at first. He was Jesus, but somehow a more glorified version of himself. In this, he is showing us what life after death will be like for those who follow him. God "is not God of the dead, but of the living." Like Jesus at Easter, we too are fully alive in him, now and forever.

......ON THE WAY TO MASS

What does the word *resurrection* mean to you?

ON THE WAY HOME FROM MASS ......

What do you look forward to about life after death?

Living the Word

This week read John 20:19–23. Discuss as a family how Jesus is different from before he died.

November 13, 2022

Thirty-Third Sunday in Ordinary Time

Hearing the Word

Luke 21:5–11

In the name of the Father, and of the Son, and of the Holy Spirit.

While some people were speaking about how the temple was adorned with costly stones and votive offerings, Jesus said, "All that you see here—the days will come when there will not be left a stone upon another stone that will not be thrown down."

Then they asked him, "Teacher, when will this happen? And what sign will there be when all these things are about to happen? He answered, "See that you not be deceived, for many will come in my name, saying, 'I am he,' and 'The time has come.' Do not follow them! When you hear of wars and insurrections, do not be terrified; for such things must happen first, but it will not immediately be the end." Then he said to them, "Nation will rise against nation, and kingdom against kingdom. There will be powerful earthquakes, famines, and plagues from place to place; and awesome sights and mighty signs will come from the sky."

Reflecting on the Word

Today's Gospel can be very confusing and overwhelming.
People want to know how they will know the end of time
is near. Jesus says that others will say, "I am he," but we are
not to follow them. How, then, are we to know when it is
him? We must learn to recognize his voice. Is there someone
you have spent so much time with that you could close your
eyes and pick that person out of a crowded room from the
sound of their voice? That is the goal for our relationship with
Jesus. Spend enough time with him that we can find him
amidst the crowd of noise. All the details of the end of the
world are less scary when we have Jesus as our beacon of
light guiding our path.

. . . . . . ON THE WAY TO MASS

Jesus wants us to only follow him. What are some ways that you
can follow Jesus every day?

ON THE WAY HOME FROM MASS . . . . . .

How can you recognize Jesus from all the false voices in the world
telling us what to do?

Living the Word

The parable of the Good Shepherd speaks about following
Jesus and recognizing his voice. This week spend time as a
family reading John 10:3b–5, 10b–11, 14–16 and pondering
what it means to recognize the voice of the Good Shepherd.

Solemnity of Our Lord Jesus Christ, King of the Universe

Hearing the Word

Luke 23:35–43

In the name of the Father, and of the Son, and of the Holy Spirit.

The people stood by and watched; the rulers, meanwhile, sneered at Jesus and said, "He saved others, let him save himself if he is the chosen one, the Messiah of God." Even the soldiers jeered at him. As they approached to offer him wine they called out, "If you are King of the Jews, save yourself." Above him there was an inscription that read, "This is the King of the Jews."

Now one of the criminals hanging there reviled Jesus, saying, "Are you not the Messiah? Save yourself and us." The other, however, rebuking him, said in reply, "Have you no fear of God, for you are subject to the same condemnation? And indeed, we have been condemned justly, for the sentence we received corresponds to our crimes, but this man has done nothing criminal." Then he said, "Jesus, remember me when you come into your kingdom." He replied to him, "Amen, I say to you, today you will be with me in Paradise."

Reflecting on the Word

Today, we celebrate Jesus Christ our King. It is interesting that on this day we read about the moments before his death, how he was mocked and humiliated, as we celebrate his kingship. Jesus is not the type of king that has lived his life in a palace and been served. He is the type of king that was born where animals live, worked throughout his life, served the sick and poor, and then gruesomely died like a criminal. But Jesus then rose from the dead to bring us new life in him. This king lived like his people so that we may always know that whatever we are going through, whatever pain we are feeling, he understands. God allowed it to happen because "God so loved the world that he gave his only Son" (John 3:16, NRSV). What a king we have!

•••••• ON THE WAY TO MASS

Today, we celebrate Jesus as King of the Universe. What does that mean that he is "King of the Universe"? What other names would you like to give Jesus?

ON THE WAY HOME FROM MASS ••••••

How do you think Jesus felt as the rulers, soldiers, and one of the criminals sneered and mocked him? Do you think it was difficult for him? What kind of king does this story tell us Jesus is?

Living the Word

Provide blank paper and pencils or crayons and allow everyone in the family to draw a picture in response to today's Gospel. It doesn't have to be a picture only of this story but anything to ponder more what was read.

November 27, 2022

First Sunday of Advent

Hearing the Word

Matthew 24:37–44

In the name of the Father, and of the Son, and of the Holy Spirit.

Jesus said to his disciples, "For as it was in the days of Noah, so it will be at the coming of the Son of Man. In those days before the flood, they were eating and drinking, marrying and giving in marriage, up to the day that Noah entered the ark. They did not know until the flood came and carried them all away. So will it be also at the coming of the Son of Man. Two men will be out in the field; one will be taken, and one will be left. Two women will be grinding at the mill; one will be taken, and one will be left. Therefore, stay awake! For you do not know on which day your Lord will come. Be sure of this: if the master of the house had known the hour of night when the thief was coming, he would have stayed awake and not let his house be broken into. So too, you also must be prepared, for at an hour you do not expect, the Son of Man will come."

Reflecting on the Word

Advent is a time to prepare our hearts to celebrate not only the day Jesus was born two thousand years ago, but also to prepare for Jesus to come again! Are we ready? Like the people before the flood, the men in the field, or the women grinding at the mill, we do not know when he will come again. But we must always be ready! How do we do this? We must always keep our eyes and hearts turned toward God for we do not know the moment when Jesus will come, and we do not want to be suddenly found looking away from him. Jesus is the way, the truth, and the life. May we recommit ourselves during this season of Advent to daily turn our eyes toward him.

......ON THE WAY TO MASS

What can we do to prepare ourselves for Jesus to come again, even though we do not know when that will be?

ON THE WAY HOME FROM MASS ......

What did you notice in the church environment today?

Living the Word

This week, set up a special Advent place in your home using a purple cloth, candles, and a wreath. For the next four weeks, try to gather as a family daily to focus on preparing your hearts for Jesus. "O Come, O Come Emmanuel" is a great Advent song to sing together.

December 4, 2022

Second Sunday of Advent

Hearing the Word

Matthew 3:1–11

In the name of the Father, and of the Son, and of the Holy Spirit.

John the Baptist appeared, preaching in the desert of Judea and saying, "Repent, for the kingdom of heaven is at hand!" It was of him that the prophet Isaiah had spoken when he said: / *A voice of one crying out in the desert, / Prepare the way of the Lord, / make straight his paths.* / John wore clothing made of camel's hair and had a leather belt around his waist. His food was locusts and wild honey. At that time Jerusalem, all Judea, and the whole region around the Jordan were going out to him and were being baptized by him in the Jordan River as they acknowledged their sins.

When he saw many of the Pharisees and Sadducees coming to his baptism, he said to them, "You brood of vipers! Who warned you to flee from the coming wrath? Produce good fruit as evidence of your repentance. And do not presume to say to yourselves, 'We have Abraham as our father.' For I tell you, God can raise up children to Abraham from these stones. Even now the ax lies at the root of the trees. Therefore every tree that does not bear good fruit will be cut down and thrown into the fire. I am baptizing you with water, for repentance, but the one who is coming after me is mightier than I. I am not worthy to carry his sandals. He will baptize you with the Holy Spirit and fire."

Reflecting on the Word

John the Baptist tells us in today's Gospel to: "Repent, for the kingdom of heaven is at hand!" and he recalls the words of Isaiah when he says, "Prepare the way of the Lord, make straight his path." John the Baptist is reminding us what this season of Advent is all about: preparation. It is easy to get distracted by all the physical preparations for Christmas, but John the Baptist is reminding us to prepare our hearts for Jesus. We remember that Jesus came into this world over two thousand years ago but we are also waiting for him to come again! If this is truly what we believe then we must prepare! We must prepare our hearts, minds, and our souls so that when Jesus comes, he find us ready and waiting for him! What a gift that will be for him!

......ON THE WAY TO MASS

Reflect silently on the mystery of God becoming man and how he will come again. Listen to the proclamation of the Gospel at Mass and think about why we need to pay attention to John's words.

ON THE WAY HOME FROM MASS ......

What does the word *repent* mean? Why is this important as we prepare for Jesus to come?

Living the Word

As a family, take advantage of the sacrament of reconciliation during this Advent season. Many parishes offer Advent reconciliation services. If the time doesn't work for you, look up the scheduled time for weekly confessions at your parish. Take the whole family so that you can be witnesses to one another of God's mercy and love.

December 8, 2022

Solemnity of the Immaculate Conception of the Blessed Virgin Mary

Hearing the Word
Luke 1:26–35

In the name of the Father, and of the Son, and of the Holy Spirit.

The angel Gabriel was sent from God to a town of Galilee called Nazareth, to a virgin betrothed to a man named Joseph, of the house of David, and the virgin's name was Mary. And coming to her, he said, "Hail, full of grace! The Lord is with you." But she was greatly troubled at what was said and pondered what sort of greeting this might be. Then the angel said to her, "Do not be afraid, Mary, for you have found favor with God. Behold, you will conceive in your womb and bear a son, and you shall name him Jesus. He will be great and will be called Son of the Most High, and the Lord God will give him the throne of David his father, and he will rule over the house of Jacob forever, and of his kingdom there will be no end." But Mary said to the angel, "How can this be, since I have no relations with a man?" And the angel said to her in reply, "The Holy Spirit will come upon you, and the power of the Most High will overshadow you. Therefore the child to be born will be called holy, the Son of God."

Reflecting on the Word

On today's feast of the Immaculate Conception, we recognize that Mary, the mother of Jesus, was sinless from the moment she was conceived in her mother's womb. God chose Mary from all women throughout time to be the mother of his Son. The angel Gabriel calls Jesus "great," "holy," "Son of the Most High," ruler over the house of Jacob forever, and "Son of God." All of these are supersize descriptors for a tiny baby. But this baby is so important that the woman who carried him must be immaculate, without sin. Today, we honor Mary, who was made perfect by God because his Son was so important that he needed a perfect dwelling place.

·······ON THE WAY TO MASS

I wonder how Mary felt when she heard the angel greet her, "Hail, full of grace! The Lord is with you."

ON THE WAY HOME FROM MASS ······

What does today's Gospel reveal to us about Jesus?

Living the Word

The annunciation is the first of the Joyful Mysteries of the Rosary. As a family this week, gather to pray this one mystery together. Start by reading today's Gospel again. Then pray an Our Father, ten Hail Marys, and finish with the Glory Be. Encourage everyone to ponder today's Gospel while repeating the Hail Marys. After the prayers are finished, share what came to mind about this Scripture passage while praying.

THIRD SUNDAY OF ADVENT

Hearing the Word
Matthew 11:2–6

In the name of the Father, and of the Son, and of the Holy Spirit.

When John the Baptist heard in prison of the works of the Christ, he sent his disciples to Jesus with this question, "Are you the one who is to come, or should we look for another?" Jesus said to them in reply, "Go and tell John what you hear and see: the blind regain their sight, the lame walk, lepers are cleansed, the deaf hear, the dead are raised, and the poor have the good news proclaimed to them. And blessed is the one who takes no offense at me."

Reflecting on the Word

Advent is a season of waiting. Waiting for Jesus' birth. Waiting for Jesus to come again. Hundreds of years before Jesus was born, prophets told how the Messiah would be born and what he would do. The people were watching and waiting for those signs to know when the Messiah had come. Isaiah, a prophet, said that the Messiah would make "the eyes of the blind shall be opened and the ears of the deaf unstopped" (Isaiah 35:5, NRSV). Jesus knew that these signs were what the people were waiting for and would help them understand who he is. How they must have felt when they realized they didn't have to wait any longer for the Savior!

• • • • • • ON THE WAY TO MASS

Who were the people who waited for the coming of the Messiah over two thousand years ago? Are you also waiting for Jesus?

ON THE WAY HOME FROM MASS • • • • • •

Jesus was able to make blind people see and lame people walk. What does this reveal to us about who Jesus is?

Living the Word

Jesus cared for many who were poor and forgotten. As a family this week, find a way to care for someone who is poor or forgotten in your area. Do you have an elderly neighbor to visit? Could you volunteer time or contribute to a food pantry? Your children may want to write a letter or draw a picture for someone to let them know that they are loved and not forgotten. Whom can you bring the love of Christ to this week?

December 18, 2022

Fourth Sunday of Advent

Hearing the Word

Matthew 1:18–24

In the name of the Father, and of the Son, and of the Holy Spirit.

This is how the birth of Jesus Christ came about. When his mother Mary was betrothed to Joseph, but before they lived together, she was found with child through the Holy Spirit. Joseph her husband, since he was a righteous man, yet unwilling to expose her to shame, decided to divorce her quietly. Such was his intention when, behold, the angel of the Lord appeared to him in a dream and said, "Joseph, son of David, do not be afraid to take Mary your wife into your home. For it is through the Holy Spirit that this child has been conceived in her. She will bear a son and you are to name him Jesus, because he will save his people from their sins." All this took place to fulfill what the Lord had said through the prophet: / *Behold, the virgin shall be with child and bear a son, / and they shall name him Emmanuel,* / which means "God is with us." When Joseph awoke, he did as the angel of the Lord had commanded him and took his wife into his home.

Reflecting on the Word

In today's Gospel, we hear Matthew's account of the birth of Jesus. In this story we see more of the person Joseph, the foster father of Jesus. We see his generosity when he wants to divorce Mary quietly so that she will not be humiliated. We see his lineage when he is called the "son of David," showing him as relative to King David. We see that he is obedient to what the angel has commanded him. Joseph, like Mary, has been chosen by God to be entrusted with God's Son. Even though Joseph has no recorded words throughout the Bible, he is a strong example to us as Christians of obedience and trustworthiness. St. Joseph, pray for us!

•••••• ON THE WAY TO MASS

Name some things you know about St. Joseph.

ON THE WAY HOME FROM MASS ••••••

The angel refers to Jesus as *Emmanuel*, which means "God is with us." Why is this a good name for Jesus?

Living the Word

Jesus and Mary both have many names given to them. But what about Joseph? As a family, do some research about names for Joseph. Make a card to add to your prayer table with some of your favorite names for Joseph written beautifully on it.

Solemnity of the Nativity of the Lord (Mass during the Night)

Hearing the Word

Luke 2:1–7a, 8–14

In the name of the Father, and of the Son, and of the Holy Spirit.

In those days a decree went out from Caesar Augustus that the whole world should be enrolled. This was the first enrollment, when Quirinius was governor of Syria. So all went to be enrolled, each to his own town. And Joseph too went up from Galilee from the town of Nazareth to Judea, to the city of David that is called Bethlehem, because he was of the house and family of David, to be enrolled with Mary, his betrothed, who was with child. While they were there, the time came for her to have her child, and she gave birth to her firstborn son.

Now there were shepherds in that region living in the fields and keeping the night watch over their flock. The angel of the Lord appeared to them and the glory of the Lord shone around them, and they were struck with great fear. The angel said to them, "Do not be afraid; for behold, I proclaim to you good news of great joy that will be for all the people. For today in the city of David a savior has been born for you who is Messiah and Lord. And this will be a sign for you: you will find an infant wrapped in swaddling clothes and lying in a manger." And suddenly there was a multitude of the heavenly host with the angel, praising God and saying: / "Glory to God in the highest / and on earth peace to those on whom his favor rests."

Reflecting on the Word

Glory to God in the highest! When Jesus was born angels rejoiced, a star shone brightly in the sky, both Jewish shepherds and non-Jewish wise men came to adore him, and Jesus, the long-awaited Messiah, was lying in a feeding place for animals. God chose a young woman named Mary to be his mother, and a small town called Bethlehem as a place for his Son to be born as a vulnerable baby. God's Son could have come to us as a strong king, with earthly power and influence, but God choose to come as a baby. Small and vulnerable must not mean the same thing to God! This baby wrapped in swaddling clothes is the Prince of Peace, Mighty God, Wonderful Counselor!

......ON THE WAY TO MASS

Why do you think God's messengers chose to make this announcement to shepherds and not to rich or powerful people?

ON THE WAY HOME FROM MASS ......

The angels sang, "Glory to God in the highest." We proclaim these same words every Sunday at Mass. I wonder how the angels felt that made them sing these words.

Living the Word

Now that the Christmas season has officially begun, change your prayer tablecloth from a purple cloth to a white one. If you received any Christmas cards that have beautiful pictures of the Nativity, display them as prayer cards on your table.

Solemnity of Mary, the Holy Mother of God

Hearing the Word

Luke 2:16–21

In the name of the Father, and of the Son, and of the Holy Spirit.

The shepherds went in haste to Bethlehem and found Mary and Joseph, and the infant lying in the manger. When they saw this, they made known the message that had been told them about this child. All who heard it were amazed by what had been told them by the shepherds. And Mary kept all these things, reflecting on them in her heart. Then the shepherds returned, glorifying and praising God for all they had heard and seen, just as it had been told to them.

When eight days were completed for his circumcision, he was named Jesus, the name given him by the angel before he was conceived in the womb.

Reflecting on the Word

Mary was the first Christian, the first to believe that Jesus was the Messiah. She had an intimate perspective of the incarnation as God took on human form inside her body. As Jesus' mother, she loved him in a unique way that only a mother can. As miraculous and surprising things happened around her son, she reflected on these moments in her heart. Mary models for us how to be a Christian as everything she does points to her son. She lived her life loving him and guiding others toward him. How much of our own lives are focused on Jesus?

• • • • • • ON THE WAY TO MASS

I wonder how Mary felt when shepherds who were strangers arrived not long after her son was born to adore him.

ON THE WAY HOME FROM MASS • • • • • •

The shepherds went in haste to find the baby. What would your reaction be after finding out about the birth of the Messiah?

Living the Word

This week have each member of your family write a letter to Mary. In their letters, they can be free to express themselves: ask questions or relay thoughts. For those unable to write yet, have them draw a picture about Mary to give to her. Take your letters and drawings to a statue of Mary at your church. Ask Mary to pray for your family as you leave her your gifts.

January 8, 2023

Solemnity of the Epiphany of the Lord

Hearing the Word
Matthew 2:1–5, 7–11

In the name of the Father, and of the Son, and of the Holy Spirit.

When Jesus was born in Bethlehem of Judea, in the days of
King Herod, behold, magi from the east arrived in Jerusalem,
saying, "Where is the newborn king of the Jews? We saw his
star at its rising and have come to do him homage." When
King Herod heard this, he was greatly troubled, and all
Jerusalem with him. Assembling all the chief priests and the
scribes of the people, he inquired of them where the Messiah
was to be born. They said to him, "In Bethlehem of Judea . . ."
Then Herod called the magi secretly and ascertained from
them the time of the star's appearance. He sent them to
Bethlehem and said, "Go and search diligently for the child.
When you have found him, bring me word, that I too may go
and do him homage." After their audience with the king they
set out. And behold, the star that they had seen at its rising
preceded them, until it came and stopped over the place where
the child was. They were overjoyed at seeing the star, and on
entering the house they saw the child with Mary his mother.
They prostrated themselves and did him homage. Then they
opened their treasures and offered him gifts of gold, frankincense, and myrrh.

Reflecting on the Word

The Magi were not Jewish, but they came and offered gifts to this child, lowering themselves in adoration before Jesus because they knew *who* he was. Their gifts give us clues into their mysterious knowledge about Jesus. Gold is a sign of kingship, frankincense is a sign of God's presence, and myrrh which was used at burials is a sign of Jesus' forthcoming sacrifice for the whole world. The Epiphany of the Lord is an important feast because it reminds us that Jesus came for all people—then and for all time.

······ ON THE WAY TO MASS

I wonder how the Magi felt after traveling for so long, following a star, then finally finding what they were looking for.

ON THE WAY HOME FROM MASS ······

Right after Jesus was born, he was adored by poor shepherds. Later, he was adored by wealthy, educated Magi. What does this tell us about Jesus and his mission?

Living the Word

The Magi came bearing gifts as an offering to the Savior. As a family, put together care packages that you can keep in your car to distribute to anyone in need. Ask your children to help with ideas on what the packages will contain: gift certificates for food? Bottles of water or snack packs? Or blankets or warm gloves? Offer them as gifts remembering that Jesus came for all people.

SECOND SUNDAY IN ORDINARY TIME

Hearing the Word

John 1:29–34

In the name of the Father, and of the Son, and of the Holy Spirit.

John the Baptist saw Jesus coming toward him and said, "Behold, the Lamb of God, who takes away the sin of the world. He is the one of whom I said, 'A man is coming after me who ranks ahead of me because he existed before me.' I did not know him, but the reason why I came baptizing with water was that he might be made known to Israel." John testified further, saying, "I saw the Spirit come down like a dove from the sky and remain upon him. I did not know him, but the one who sent me to baptize with water told me, 'On whomever you see the Spirit come down and remain, he is the one who will baptize with the Holy Spirit.' Now I have seen and testified that he is the Son of God."

Reflecting on the Word

Today, we hear another name for Jesus: "Lamb of God."
We have heard about Jesus the Good Shepherd who calls his
sheep by name and they follow him. Today, however, we hear
that he is not only the shepherd, but also the lamb. During
the Passover in Egypt, the Jewish people offered a sacrifice
of a lamb so that they would be saved. Jesus became the
sacrificial lamb, the lamb that offers his whole self so that
we may be saved and live eternally with him in heaven. Jesus,
the Son of God, the Prince of Peace, the Light of the World,
is also the "Lamb of God who takes away the sins of the
world." What love he has for us that he is both our shepherd
and our sacrificial lamb.

......ON THE WAY TO MASS

Today we hear John the Baptist's words "Behold, the Lamb of
God, who takes away the sins of the world." We also hear these
words during Mass when the priest is holding the Body of Christ.
What does this tell us about the Eucharist if these are the words
spoken while lifting up the host?

ON THE WAY HOME FROM MASS ......

Who was John the Baptist? What kind of person was he? How can
he be a good example to us on how to grow closer to God?

Living the Word

There are many beautiful artworks of the *Agnus Dei* or
"Lamb of God." As a family search online for some of the
images and reflect on what you see. What might the image
be trying to convey through the symbols used?

THIRD SUNDAY IN ORDINARY TIME

Hearing the Word

Matthew 4:13–22

In the name of the Father, and of the Son, and of the Holy Spirit.

[Jesus] left Nazareth and went to live in Capernaum by the sea, in the region of Zebulun and Naphtali, that what had been said through Isaiah the prophet might be fulfilled: / *Land of Zebulun and land of Naphtali, / the way to the sea, beyond the Jordan, / Galilee of the Gentiles, / the people who sit in darkness have seen a great light, / on those dwelling in a land overshadowed by death / light has arisen.* / From that time on, Jesus began to preach and say, "Repent, for the kingdom of heaven is at hand."

As he was walking by the Sea of Galilee, he saw two brothers, Simon who is called Peter, and his brother Andrew, casting a net into the sea; they were fishermen. He said to them, "Come after me, and I will make you fishers of men." At once they left their nets and followed him. He walked along from there and saw two other brothers, James, the son of Zebedee, and his brother John. They were in a boat, with their father Zebedee, mending their nets. He called them, and immediately they left their boat and their father and followed him.

Reflecting on the Word

Today, we hear about the beginning of Jesus' public ministry. Jesus comes upon two sets of brothers and he calls them. They immediately follow him. These men go where Jesus goes, learn from him, sometimes get his lessons wrong, sometimes get it right, and even momentarily disown Jesus when things are at its worst. Yet they didn't give up. This is their story of following Jesus. Perhaps it is our story too. We have been called, but what has our discipleship looked like? We can find comfort in how the apostles walked with Jesus, knowing that following him is full of ups and downs, full of missteps, but each day Jesus is calling us, too. Are we going to drop our nets and follow him?

•••••• ON THE WAY TO MASS

Do you think it is difficult to leave everything to follow Jesus?

ON THE WAY HOME FROM MASS ••••••

When Jesus called the first disciples to follow him, I wonder how they felt.

Living the Word

Many people throughout history have responded to Jesus' call to follow him and make fishers of men. The saints are wonderful examples to us of this response. Throughout this week read the lives of a few saints to inspire your family in your journey to follow Jesus.

January 29, 2023

Fourth Sunday in Ordinary Time

Hearing the Word

Matthew 5:1–12

In the name of the Father, and of the Son, and of the Holy Spirit.

[Jesus said]: "Blessed are the poor in spirit, / for theirs is the kingdom of heaven. / Blessed are they who mourn, / for they will be comforted. / Blessed are the meek, / for they will inherit the land. / Blessed are they who hunger and thirst for righteousness, / for they will be satisfied. / Blessed are the merciful, / for they will be shown mercy. / Blessed are the clean of heart, / for they will see God. / Blessed are the peacemakers, / for they will be called children of God. / Blessed are they who are persecuted for the sake of righteousness, / for theirs is the kingdom of heaven. / Blessed are you when they insult you and persecute you / and utter every kind of evil against you [falsely] because of me. / Rejoice and be glad, / for your reward will be great in heaven."

Reflecting on the Word

The list in today's Gospel is called the Beatitudes. The word *Beatitude* means "blessedness," or "happiness." Just like Jesus tends to do, he takes what most scorn or see as a burden and call it blessed. Those who mourn, who are meek, or who show mercy are blessed because God is with those who need him. Being poor in spirit is not about having a weak spirit but rather knowing that you need God, recognizing that all that you have comes from him and not from yourself. Jesus desires for us to make him the center of our lives and recognize that everything else flows out of his abundant love for us.

. . . . . . ON THE WAY TO MASS

In what ways are you blessed by God?

ON THE WAY HOME FROM MASS . . . . . .

Which Beatitude do you find most challenging? Why do you think it is hard?

Living the Word

Have your family make a list of all their blessings. Pray together thanking God, as he is the source of each of these blessings. Throughout the week, have members add to the list as they recognize more blessings in their lives.

February 5, 2023

Fifth Sunday in Ordinary Time

Hearing the Word

Matthew 5:13–16

In the name of the Father, and of the Son, and of the Holy Spirit.

Jesus said to his disciples: "You are the salt of the earth. But if salt loses its taste, with what can it be seasoned? It is no longer good for anything but to be thrown out and trampled underfoot. You are the light of the world. A city set on a mountain cannot be hidden. Nor do they light a lamp and then put it under a bushel basket; it is set on a lampstand, where it gives light to all in the house. Just so, your light must shine before others, that they may see your good deeds and glorify your heavenly Father."

Reflecting on the Word

Being a Christian is not passive. We cannot sit and watch the world and not be a part of it. As Christians we are called to be the "salt of the earth" and the "light of the world." Salt is not made to sit in a bowl and never be used. Its purpose is to be added to food for flavor. Light also is meant to push away the darkness. Jesus calls us to take the light that we have received from his love and let it touch every part of our life and the lives of those around us. We are called to bring flavor, to transform the darkness into light with our lives.

······ ON THE WAY TO MASS

What does salt do to food? What could Jesus be asking of us when he calls us to be the salt of the earth?

ON THE WAY HOME FROM MASS ······

What happens to a light placed under a bushel basket? What if light is placed on a lampstand? If our light is the love of Jesus that he has given us, what might he want us to do with it?

Living the Word

Reread today's Gospel together with this visual: light a candle and place it under a basket. With the lights in the room off, ask your family to share what they observe about the light. Then remove the candle from under the basket and place it on a counter or footrest or table and share your observations again. What new insights does anyone have about the Gospel when they see what happens to the lit candle?

February 12, 2023

Sixth Sunday in Ordinary Time

Hearing the Word

Matthew 5:21–22a, 27–28, 33–34a, 37

In the name of the Father, and of the Son, and of the Holy Spirit.

[Jesus said to his disciples:] "You have heard that it was said to your ancestors, *You shall not kill; and whoever kills will be liable to judgment.* But I say to you, whoever is angry with his brother will be liable to judgment.

"You have heard that it was said, *You shall not commit adultery.* But I say to you, everyone who looks at a woman with lust has already committed adultery with her in his heart.

"Again, you have heard that it was said to your ancestors, *Do not take a false oath, but make good to the Lord all that you vow.* But I say to you, do not swear at all. Let your 'Yes' mean 'Yes,' and your 'No' mean 'No.' Anything more is from the evil one."

Reflecting on the Word

Today's Gospel is an excerpt from Jesus' Sermon on the Mount. He restates commandments but calls us to take them even further. They are not about following the rules God has laid before us but about living in wisdom and truth that will set us free. If our focus is on following the rules, we have lost the point. If our focus is on loving God, our neighbor, and ourselves then we have embraced the heart of what Jesus is calling us to. The commandments are no longer about what we are "supposed" to do or not supposed to do, but about truly loving with our whole selves. This is the deeper conversion Jesus longs for us to have.

......ON THE WAY TO MASS

Can you name the Ten Commandments? Why did God give us these commandments?

ON THE WAY HOME FROM MASS ......

Jesus tells us to let our "yes mean yes" and our "no mean no." Do you ever say yes to something but do not follow through? Why do you think following through is important to God?

Living the Word

This week come up with some commandments for your family. Try and think of what will call the members of your family to a deeper love of God, one another, and themselves. Write or print them to be beautifully displayed in your home for your family to see regularly.

February 19, 2023

Seventh Sunday in Ordinary Time

Hearing the Word

Matthew 5:38–48

In the name of the Father, and of the Son, and of the Holy Spirit.

Jesus said to his disciples, "You have heard that it was said, *An eye for an eye and a tooth for a tooth.* But I say to you, offer no resistance to the one who is evil. When someone strikes you on [your] right cheek, turn the other one to him as well. If anyone wants to go to law with you over your tunic, hand him your cloak as well. Should anyone press you into service for one mile, go with him for two miles. Give to the one who asks of you, and do not turn your back on one who wants to borrow.

"You have heard that it was said, *You shall love your neighbor and hate your enemy.* But I say to you, love your enemies, and pray for those who persecute you, that you may be children of your heavenly Father, for he makes his sun rise on the bad and the good, and causes rain to fall on the just and the unjust. For if you love those who love you, what recompense will you have? Do not the tax collectors do the same? And if you greet your brothers only, what is unusual about that? Do not the pagans do the same? So be perfect, just as your heavenly Father is perfect."

Reflecting on the Word

Forgiving and loving your enemies are hard, but we are all sinners. We have made mistakes many times throughout our lives. We have turned our back on the love of God to try and make ourselves happy, and it never works. Yet Jesus forgives us. On the cross Jesus said, "Forgive them, Father, for they know not what they do." As Jesus was in agony, dying for our sins, he wanted us to be forgiven. Jesus is a model for us. There is not a person on earth that God will not forgive for anything. So there is not a person on earth that we should not forgive also. Forgiveness is hard, but then again, Jesus never said that following him would be easy.

•••••• ON THE WAY TO MASS

Is there someone in your life that you are having a hard time forgiving? Have you spoken with God about it?

ON THE WAY HOME FROM MASS ••••••

How does Jesus show love and forgiveness in his own life? Why do you think this is so important to him?

Living the Word

As a family, reflect on a past hurt. Allow those who want to share the time to do so. Then as a family pray for each of these people by name. How do you feel afterward? Ask God to help you pray for this person regularly.

February 26, 2023

First Sunday of Lent

Hearing the Word
Matthew 4:1–4

In the name of the Father, and of the Son, and of the Holy Spirit.

Jesus was led by the Spirit into the desert to be tempted by the devil. He fasted for forty days and forty nights, and afterwards he was hungry. The tempter approached and said to him, "If you are the Son of God, command that these stones become loaves of bread." He said in reply, "It is written: *One does not live by bread alone, / but on every word that comes forth / from the mouth of God.*"

Reflecting on the Word

In today's Gospel, Jesus went to the desert and was tempted by the devil. This fact alone reveals so much to us. Our Savior understands the feeling of temptation. He knows it is not easy. Because our sinless Savior was indeed tempted, we can see also that temptation itself is not a sin. Sometimes we may feel guilty for being tempted to sin and the shame of that guilt makes us want to run from God. But in these moments of temptation, running toward God is where we will find strength and comfort. During these forty days of Lent, may our prayers and fasting strengthen our faith and relationship with God so that we may be able to fight temptation as Jesus did in the desert.

......ON THE WAY TO MASS

What are common temptations in your life? Do you lean on God in times of temptation?

ON THE WAY HOME FROM MASS ......

Jesus fasted from food for forty days in the desert. What will you be fasting from this Lent?

Living the Word

Assign each member of your family another family member to pray for throughout this week. Pray for them to have Jesus' strength during moments of temptations.

Now that we have begun Lent, change your family prayer tablecloth to a purple one, the color of preparation, as we spend this season preparing for Easter!

March 5, 2023

Second Sunday of Lent

Hearing the Word
Matthew 17:1–8

In the name of the Father, and of the Son, and of the Holy Spirit.

Jesus took Peter, James, and John his brother, and led them up a high mountain by themselves. And he was transfigured before them; his face shone like the sun and his clothes became white as light. And behold, Moses and Elijah appeared to them, conversing with him. Then Peter said to Jesus in reply, "Lord, it is good that we are here. If you wish, I will make three tents here, one for you, one for Moses, and one for Elijah." While he was still speaking, behold, a bright cloud cast a shadow over them, then from the cloud came a voice that said, "This is my beloved Son, with whom I am well pleased; listen to him." When the disciples heard this, they fell prostrate and were very much afraid. But Jesus came and touched them, saying, "Rise, and do not be afraid." And when the disciples raised their eyes, they saw no one else but Jesus alone.

Reflecting on the Word

In the Bible, many significant moments with God happen on mountain tops. For example, Moses received the Ten Commandments on Mount Sinai and Jesus gave us the Beatitudes preaching on high. In today's Gospel, we hear that instead of a revelation being given, Jesus is the revelation. Jesus has been walking with his disciples for three years teaching them and performing miracles in front of them, but they still did not understand fully who he was. On this mountain top Jesus is transfigured before them and God tells them, "This is my beloved Son." Jesus reveals his full nature as not only fully human but also fully divine. Jesus is truly God! What a revelation he is!

••••••ON THE WAY TO MASS

Why do you think God said, "This is my beloved Son, with whom I am well pleased; listen to him."

ON THE WAY HOME FROM MASS ••••••

What does today's Gospel reveal to you about who Jesus is?

Living the Word

Have your children draw a picture of Jesus and then put a flashlight behind the picture to see what he would look like with his face shining like the sun and his clothes white as light.

THIRD SUNDAY OF LENT

Hearing the Word

John 4:6–10, 25–26, 39, 41–42

In the name of the Father, and of the Son, and of the Holy Spirit.

Jesus, tired about his journey, sat down there at the well. It was about noon.

A woman of Samaria came to draw water. Jesus said to her, "Give me a drink." His disciples had gone into the town to buy food. The Samaritan woman said to him, "How can you, a Jew, ask me, a Samaritan woman, for a drink?"— For Jews use nothing in common with Samaritans.— Jesus answered and said to her, "If you knew the gift of God and who is saying to you, 'Give me a drink,' you would have asked him and he would have given you living water."

The woman said to him, "I know that the Messiah is coming, the one called the Christ; when he comes, he will tell us everything." Jesus said to her, "I am he, the one who is speaking with you."

Many of the Samaritans of that town began to believe in him because of the word of the woman who testified, "He told me everything I have done." Many more began to believe in him because of his word, and they said to the woman, "We no longer believe because of your word; for we have heard for ourselves, and we know that this is truly the savior of the world."

Reflecting on the Word

Every human being desires to feel loved, seen, and wanted. The Samaritan woman is no different. The full text reveals that she searched for love and acceptance in the wrong places. Yet God is so good. Jesus knew her before he met her. He sat by the well waiting for her to come to draw water. He saw right into her heart, into her hurts and desires. He invited her to embrace the gift of "living water" that only he can give—the "living water" that would make her feel loved, seen, and wanted as she so desperately desired. God's love bubbled over so much inside her that she had to share it. She immediately told others about him, desiring for them to experience what she was experiencing.

......ON THE WAY TO MASS

How might the Samaritan woman have felt as she was walking to the well at the beginning of the story? How do you think she felt after meeting Jesus?

ON THE WAY HOME FROM MASS ......

Jesus calls himself the "living water." What do you think Jesus meant by *living* water?

Living the Word

As a family, reflect on all the ways that water helps you in your life. Throughout the week, as you use water, reflect together on how Jesus is like water. How is he the *living* water?

March 19, 2023

Fourth Sunday of Lent

Hearing the Word
John 9:1–3, 6–7

In the name of the Father, and of the Son, and of the Holy Spirit.

As Jesus passed by he saw a man blind from birth. His disciples
asked him, "Rabbi, who sinned, this man or his parents,
that he was born blind?" Jesus answered, "Neither he nor
his parents sinned; it is so that the works of God might be
made visible through him." When he had said this, he spat
on the ground and made clay with the saliva, and smeared
the clay on his eyes, and said to him, "Go wash in the Pool
of Siloam"—which means Sent—. So he went and washed,
and came back able to see.

Reflecting on the Word

In Genesis we are told that God created us in his "image and likeness." When God created people of different sizes, he created them in his image. When God created people of different colors, he created them in his image. When God created people of different abilities: deaf, blind, autistic, ADD, dyslexic, and so on, he created them in his image. God does not make mistakes. When God created each human being he said, "It is very good." Every part of what makes them who they are is "very good." God has a plan to use each of us to build his Kingdom and he needs our unique looks, personalities, and abilities to do that. God made you exactly as you are so that "the works of God might be made visible" through *you*! Praise God for *you*, exactly as you are.

•••••• ON THE WAY TO MASS

What are some ways that God might be made visible through you?

ON THE WAY HOME FROM MASS ••••••

I wonder how the blind man felt when Jesus said that God would be made visible through him.

Living the Word

As a family read the first story of creation, Genesis 1:1–31. Discuss words that you hear repeated and what they might mean. Discuss the difference between the creation of human beings and every other creation. What does this say about us? What does this say about you individually?

Fifth Sunday of Lent

Hearing the Word
John 11:17–23

In the name of the Father, and of the Son, and of the Holy Spirit.

When Jesus arrived, he found that Lazarus had already been in the tomb for four days. Now Bethany was near Jerusalem, only about two miles away. And many of the Jews had come to Martha and Mary to comfort them about their brother. When Martha heard that Jesus was coming, she went to meet him; but Mary sat at home. Martha said to Jesus, "Lord, if you had been here, my brother would not have died. But even now I know that whatever you ask of God, God will give you." Jesus said to her, "Your brother will rise."

Reflecting on the Word

Martha is grieving her beloved brother's death and yet she displays deep faith in Jesus. She doesn't only believe that Jesus could have saved her brother from dying, she believes he still can save him after death: "But even now I know that whatever you ask of God, God will give you." Martha recognizes that Jesus is God's own Son and therefore has the power to save life as well as to bring someone back to life. This is not a small faith, a small ask, a small miracle. Martha believes in who Jesus is and what he is capable of. She knows that nothing is impossible for God.

. . . . . . ON THE WAY TO MASS

When have you prayed for Jesus to help you with something? Did you believe that he would?

ON THE WAY HOME FROM MASS . . . . . .

I wonder how Martha was feeling before she heard Jesus was coming. I wonder how she felt after Jesus said, "Your brother will rise."

Living the Word

During this week, as a family, read the whole story of the death and raising of Lazarus: John 11:1–44. Talk about what this story reveals to us about who Jesus is.

April 2, 2023

Palm Sunday of the Passion of the Lord

Hearing the Word

Matthew 21:1–11

In the name of the Father, and of the Son, and of the Holy Spirit.

When Jesus and the disciples drew near Jerusalem and came
to Bethphage on the Mount of Olives, Jesus sent two disciples,
saying to them, "Go into the village opposite you, and immediately you will find an ass tethered, and a colt with her. Untie
them and bring them here to me. And if anyone should say
anything to you, reply, 'The master has need of them.' Then he
will send them at once." This happened so that what had been
spoken through the prophet might be fulfilled: / *Say to daughter
Zion, / "Behold, your king comes to you, / meek and riding on an
ass, / and on a colt, the foal of a beast of burden." /* The disciples
went and did as Jesus had ordered them. They brought the ass
and the colt and laid their cloaks over them, and he sat upon
them. The very large crowd spread their cloaks on the road,
while others cut branches from the trees and strewed them
on the road. The crowds preceding him and those following
kept crying out and saying: / "Hosanna to the Son of David; /
blessed is he who comes in the name of the Lord; / hosanna in
the highest." / And when he entered Jerusalem the whole city
was shaken and asked, "Who is this?" And the crowds replied,
"This is Jesus the prophet, from Nazareth in Galilee."

Reflecting on the Word

In Jesus' time, kings rode on donkeys through the streets during times of peace. Jesus' entry into Jerusalem was intentional. He had his disciples find a specific donkey to ride into Jerusalem during the great feast of Passover when the streets would be filled with people. Jesus was declaring himself a king and the one about whom the prophets wrote. He was sending a message to all who would hear it: "Behold, your king comes to you." Jesus was not like all other kings with money and a palace. He began life in a stable and labored as a carpenter. Yet he is the king who came to bring us back to the arms of his Father with love and mercy. He truly is the King of Kings, the one "who comes in the name of the Lord."

. . . . . . ON THE WAY TO MASS

Imagine yourself as one of the people in the crowd, spreading your cloak on the road for Jesus' donkey to walk on, and shouting "Hosanna" to him as he passed. Share what you might be experiencing.

ON THE WAY HOME FROM MASS . . . . . .

Hundreds of years before Jesus, the prophets wrote about the Messiah's triumphant entry into Jerusalem. What do their words tell us about Jesus?

Living the Word

This is a fun Scripture passage to reenact. As a family, divide the parts so that as one person narrates the Scripture, the others may act the story out. Get creative and have fun with it!

April 9, 2023

EASTER SUNDAY OF THE RESURRECTION OF THE LORD

Hearing the Word

Matthew 28:1–10

In the name of the Father, and of the Son, and of the Holy Spirit.

After the sabbath, as the first day of the week was dawning, Mary Magdalene and the other Mary came to see the tomb. And behold, there was a great earthquake; for an angel of the Lord descended from heaven, approached, rolled back the stone, and sat upon it. His appearance was like lightning and his clothing was white as snow. The guards were shaken with fear of him and became like dead men. Then the angel said to the women in reply, "Do not be afraid! I know that you are seeking Jesus the crucified. He is not here, for he has been raised just as he said. Come and see the place where he lay. Then go quickly and tell his disciples, 'He has been raised from the dead, and he is going before you to Galilee; there you will see him.' Behold, I have told you." Then they went away quickly from the tomb, fearful yet overjoyed, and ran to announce this to his disciples. And behold, Jesus met them on their way and greeted them. They approached, embraced his feet, and did him homage. Then Jesus said to them, "Do not be afraid. Go tell my brothers to go to Galilee, and there they will see me."

Reflecting on the Word

Today, we join with the whole Church to celebrate Easter, the greatest feast of all, the feast of Christ's rising from the dead. As the women were walking to the tomb, they were consumed with sadness for their friend and Messiah who had been killed. When they arrived, however, nothing was as they expected it. The earth shook, an angel appeared, and he proclaimed the most glorious news! Jesus was not dead. His love for us was so great, he died and then conquered death. He was alive. His light would never go out again. They were told to "Go tell" because this light is meant to be shared. That is reason to exclaim, Alleluia! Praise to the risen King!

......ON THE WAY TO MASS

Imagine you were approaching Jesus' tomb that early morning. How would you have reacted to the earthquake and the angel of the Lord descending from heaven? What would you have thought about his message?

ON THE WAY HOME FROM MASS ......

After the women were told about Jesus rising from the dead, they were told to "Go tell" this good news. How can we also "Go tell" this good news?

Living the Word

Easter is such a wonderful feast that we celebrate it for fifty days! Change your prayer tablecloth to a white one. Throughout this season sing Easter songs and read the stories about Jesus after he rose from the dead to remind your family that we are still celebrating this great feast!

April 16, 2023

Second Sunday of Easter / Sunday of Divine Mercy

Hearing the Word

John 20:19–29

In the name of the Father, and of the Son, and of the Holy Spirit.

On the evening of that first day of the week, when the doors were locked, where the disciples were, . . . Jesus came and stood in their midst and said to them, "Peace be with you." When he had said this, he showed them his hands and his side. The disciples rejoiced when they saw the Lord. Jesus said to them again, "Peace be with you. As the Father has sent me, so I send you." And when he had said this, he breathed on them and said to them, "Receive the Holy Spirit. Whose sins you forgive are forgiven them, and whose sins you retain are retained."

Thomas, called Didymus, one of the Twelve, was not with them when Jesus came. So the other disciples said to him, "We have seen the Lord." But he said to them, "Unless I see the mark of the nails in his hands and put my finger into the nailmarks and put my hand into his side, I will not believe."

Now a week later . . . Jesus came . . . and said, "Peace be with you." Then he said to Thomas, "Put your finger here and see my hands, and bring your hand and put it into my side, and do not be unbelieving, but believe." Thomas answered and said to him, "My Lord and my God!" Jesus said to him, "Have you come to believe because you have seen me? Blessed are those who have not seen and have believed."

Reflecting on the Word

Today's Gospel begins on the evening of that first Easter Sunday. The apostles have locked themselves in the room out of fear that what happened to Jesus would also happen to them. Thomas is not there with them but hears about Jesus' appearance later. He doubts what the others have told him. He wanted to see with his own eyes and touch with his own fingers before he could trust again. Jesus knows this and meets Thomas where he is. Jesus restores Thomas' trust and calls him to a deeper faith in him. This is God's divine mercy for us all. It is God meeting us where we are, like Thomas, and loving us back to fullness with him.

• • • • • • ON THE WAY TO MASS

Alert your children that they will hear a Gospel passage about St. Thomas doubting that Jesus had risen. Feeling doubt is natural sometimes in our life of faith. What is most important is what we do with our doubt. It is okay to have questions, as Thomas did. It is okay to rely on God as you seek the answers to your questions. Doubt can make your faith stronger. Encourage your children to ask what might be in their hearts about God.

ON THE WAY HOME FROM MASS • • • • • •

Jesus said, "Blessed are those who have not seen and have believed." Who are those that have believed without seeing? Is this hard or easy to do?

Living the Word

As a family look up the painting *The Incredulity of Saint Thomas* by Caravaggio. Discuss what you see and what each person in the painting might be feeling.

April 23, 2023

THIRD SUNDAY OF EASTER

Hearing the Word

Luke 24:13–15, 30–32

In the name of the Father, and of the Son, and of the Holy Spirit.

That very day, the first day of the week, two of Jesus' disciples were going to a village seven miles from Jerusalem called Emmaus, and they were conversing about all the things that had occurred. And it happened that while they were conversing and debating, Jesus himself drew near and walked with them. And it happened that, while he was with them at table, he took bread, said the blessing, broke it, and gave it to them. With that their eyes were opened and they recognized him, but he vanished from their sight. Then they said to each other, "Were not our hearts burning within us while he spoke to us on the way and opened the Scriptures to us?"

Reflecting on the Word

I wonder what it was like for these two disciples to walk, discuss, and break bread with Jesus. To listen to him discuss the Scriptures with them. To watch him take the bread, bless it, break it, and give it to them as he did during the Last Supper, and then to realize it was Jesus with them. What an experience! At Mass, we also experience what these two disciples experienced on the road to Emmaus. During the Liturgy of the Word, we hear the Scriptures proclaimed and broken open for us. During the Liturgy of the Eucharist, the bread is taken, blessed, broken, and given to us. We can experience an Emmaus moment every Sunday!

······ ON THE WAY TO MASS

In which part of the Mass is Jesus revealed to you the most? Why?

ON THE WAY HOME FROM MASS ······

At what moment did the disciples recognize who Jesus was? Why would this moment reveal that to them?

Living the Word

Sometime during this week, go for a walk as a family. Talk about what the disciples might have been wearing, what shoes they might have had, if you think the walk would have been easy for them. At some point in the walk, stop and read today's Gospel. Then discuss on the way home what it would have been like to walk and talk with Jesus on your walk!

April 30, 2023

Fourth Sunday of Easter

Hearing the Word
John 10:1–10

In the name of the Father, and of the Son, and of the Holy Spirit.

Jesus said, "Amen, amen, I say to you, whoever does not enter a sheepfold through the gate but climbs over elsewhere is a thief and a robber. But whoever enters through the gate is the shepherd of the sheep. The gatekeeper opens it for him, and the sheep hear his voice, as the shepherd calls his own sheep by name and leads them out. When he has driven out all his own, he walks ahead of them, and the sheep follow him, because they recognize his voice. But they will not follow a stranger; they will run away from him, because they do not recognize the voice of strangers." Although Jesus used this figure of speech, the Pharisees did not realize what he was trying to tell them.

So Jesus said again, "Amen, amen, I say to you, I am the gate for the sheep. All who came before me are thieves and robbers, but the sheep did not listen to them. I am the gate. Whoever enters through me will be saved, and will come in and go out and find pasture. A thief comes only to steal and slaughter and destroy; I came so that they might have life and have it more abundantly."

Reflecting on the Word

The shepherd described in today's Gospel is not like other shepherds, he is the Good Shepherd. He knows his sheep so well that he can tell them apart, he knows them each by name. The sheep have spent so much time with him that they know his voice. They recognize his voice over all other voices. This love between the Good Shepherd and his sheep is the model for all love. The Good Shepherd knows his sheep, wants them to be with him, and loves them so much he will die for them. These basic human needs to be known, wanted, and loved are universal to us all. The Good Shepherd is waiting to provide these things for us abundantly.

••••••ON THE WAY TO MASS

I wonder what it feels like for the Good Shepherd to call you by name. I wonder what it feels like to be a sheep of the Good Shepherd.

ON THE WAY HOME FROM MASS ••••••

Why do you think the sheep recognize the Good Shepherd's voice? Do you spend enough time with Jesus to recognize his voice?

Living the Word

Today's Gospel helps us ponder who Jesus is. Throughout this week, reread this Scripture passage as a family a few times to allow yourselves to really ponder the deep meanings in it. Provide blank paper and crayons so that your children can draw a response to what they have heard.

May 7, 2023

Fifth Sunday of Easter

Hearing the Word
John 14:1–10a

In the name of the Father, and of the Son, and of the Holy Spirit.

Jesus said to his disciples, "Do not let your hearts be troubled. You have faith in God; have faith also in me. In my Father's house there are many dwelling places. If there were not, would I have told you that I am going to prepare a place for you? And if I go and prepare a place for you, I will come back again and take you to myself, so that where I am you also may be. Where I am going you know the way." Thomas said to him, "Master, we do not know where you are going; how can we know the way?" Jesus said to him, "I am the way and the truth and the life. No one comes to the Father except through me. If you know me, then you will also know my Father. From now on you do know him and have seen him." Philip said to him, "Master, show us the Father, and that will be enough for us." Jesus said to him, "Have I been with you for so long a time and you still do not know me, Philip? Whoever has seen me has seen the Father. How can you say, 'Show us the Father'? Do you not believe that I am in the Father and the Father is in me?"

Reflecting on the Word

Today's Gospel takes place during the Last Supper and reveals some of Jesus' final words to his disciples. During these last moments with them he speaks those famous words, "I am the way, the truth, and the life." Throughout human history, people have always had many different paths they could choose for themselves, but here Jesus is saying he is the right path. As on all paths, however, you must pay attention so that you do not stray from it. You must know and recognize who Jesus is to know how to follow his way. When we spend time with him in Scripture and in prayer, we learn to recognize him and his truth so that our lives follow his.

······ ON THE WAY TO MASS

What are some ways that we can follow Jesus in our day-to-day lives?

ON THE WAY HOME FROM MASS ······

What does Jesus mean when he says, "I am the way"?

Living the Word

Have your children help you make signs that read: "I am the *way*, the *truth*, and the *life*." Place them in common areas, such as the bathroom mirror, front door, or microwave so that this message will be seen and read often Let these signs remind you of Jesus' words so they can be imprinted on your hearts.

May 14, 2023

Sixth Sunday of Easter

Hearing the Word
John 14:15–21

In the name of the Father, and of the Son, and of the Holy Spirit.

Jesus said to his disciples, "If you love me, you will keep my commandments. And I will ask the Father, and he will give you another Advocate to be with you always, the Spirit of truth, whom the world cannot accept, because it neither sees nor knows him. But you know him, because he remains with you, and will be in you. I will not leave you orphans; I will come to you. In a little while the world will no longer see me, but you will see me, because I live and you will live. On that day you will realize that I am in my Father and you are in me and I in you. Whoever has my commandments and observes them is the one who loves me. And whoever loves me will be loved by my Father, and I will love him and reveal myself to him."

Reflecting on the Word

What you are in love with determines everything about your life. It decides how you spend your time, what you think about, what decisions you make. When we are in love with Jesus, we desire to follow him. We desire to keep his commandments. Keeping the commandments is rooted in our relationship with the one who gave them to us. Our actions must first be rooted in our being in relationship with him; otherwise, we are following them out of fear and obligation rather than from an authentic response to God's love.

•••••• ON THE WAY TO MASS

What are ways that you can show Jesus that you love him?

ON THE WAY HOME FROM MASS ••••••

Is it difficult to keep Jesus' commandments? Is there one commandment that is harder for you to follow?

Living the Word

Jesus gave us two commandments that summarize all the commandments. Read Matthew 22:37 and Matthew 22:39, and then discuss them as a family. Which of these two commandments do you think is harder to follow?

May 18 or 21, 2023

Solemnity of the Ascension of the Lord

Hearing the Word

Matthew 28:16–20

In the name of the Father, and of the Son, and of the Holy Spirit.

The eleven disciples went to Galilee, to the mountain to which Jesus had ordered them. When they saw him, they worshiped, but they doubted. Then Jesus approached and said to them, "All power in heaven and on earth has been given to me. Go, therefore, and make disciples of all nations, baptizing them in the name of the Father, and of the Son, and of the Holy Spirit, teaching them to observe all that I have commanded you. And behold, I am with you always, until the end of the age."

Reflecting on the Word

For forty days after his resurrection, Jesus Christ would appear to his apostles. Before Jesus finally ascended to his Father, he told them to do something very important: to go make disciples of all nations. Jesus had been walking with and teaching his disciples for three years, preparing them for this moment when they would be sent out into the world. With Jesus no longer walking on the earth, it was up to all the disciples to spread his love and message. What Jesus asked of his disciples is what he also asks of us. We also are being called to go make disciples of all nations. Yet Jesus assures us that we are not alone on this mission, he will be with us always.

•••••• ON THE WAY TO MASS

What does it mean to "Go and make disciples of all nations"? Does it mean we have to travel afar? What are some ways we can answer Jesus' call?

ON THE WAY HOME FROM MASS ••••••

I wonder how the disciples felt about Jesus' words to "Go and make disciples of all nations."

Living the Word

The ascension is the second Glorious Mystery of the Rosary. As a family this week, gather to pray this mystery together. Start by reading today's Gospel again. Then pray an Our Father, ten Hail Marys, and finish with the Glory Be. Encourage everyone to ponder today's Gospel while repeating the Hail Marys. Afterward, share what came to mind about this Scripture passage while praying.

May 21, 2023

Seventh Sunday of Easter

Hearing the Word

John 17:1–11a

In the name of the Father, and of the Son, and of the Holy Spirit.

Jesus raised his eyes to heaven and said, "Father, the hour has come. Give glory to your son, so that your son may glorify you, just as you gave him authority over all people, so that he may give eternal life to all you gave him. Now this is eternal life, that they should know you, the only true God, and the one whom you sent, Jesus Christ. I glorified you on earth by accomplishing the work that you gave me to do. Now glorify me, Father, with you, with the glory that I had with you before the world began.

"I revealed your name to those whom you gave me out of the world. They belonged to you, and you gave them to me, and they have kept your word. Now they know that everything you gave me is from you, because the words you gave to me I have given to them, and they accepted them and truly understood that I came from you, and they have believed that you sent me. I pray for them. I do not pray for the world but for the ones you have given me, because they are yours, and everything of mine is yours and everything of yours is mine, and I have been glorified in them. And now I will no longer be in the world, but they are in the world, while I am coming to you."

Reflecting on the Word

Today's Gospel takes place at the Last Supper. Jesus speaks directly to his heavenly Father while his disciples listened. He says that knowing the only true God and Jesus is the only way to eternal life. Jesus speaks these words knowing that he will soon be crucified and that he has little time left with his disciples. He will die, but he will also rise again, and the eternal life he refers to is a message he wants to share with his disciples. Jesus also shares it with us, and we are to share it with anyone who knows him and accepts him.

······ ON THE WAY TO MASS

Jesus speaks to his Father in prayer often throughout the Gospel accounts. Why? How often do you speak to God? What could help you pray more often?

ON THE WAY HOME FROM MASS ······

Jesus says that knowing God and knowing Jesus will give us eternal life. What can we do to know God and Jesus more?

Living the Word

Today we hear Jesus' words spoken directly to his Father the night before he was crucified. As a family, write a letter to God. What would you want to say to him if you knew that you were going to die tomorrow?

May 28, 2023

Solemnity of Pentecost

Hearing the Word

John 20:19–23

In the name of the Father, and of the Son, and of the Holy Spirit.

On the evening of that first day of the week, when the doors were locked, where the disciples were, for fear of the Jews, Jesus came and stood in their midst and said to them, "Peace be with you." When he had said this, he showed them his hands and his side. The disciples rejoiced when they saw the Lord. Jesus said to them again, "Peace be with you. As the Father has sent me, so I send you." And when he had said this, he breathed on them and said to them, "Receive the Holy Spirit. Whose sins you forgive are forgiven them, and whose sins you retain are retained."

Reflecting on the Word

Jesus breathing on the disciples seems like such a strange thing to do, but this also happened in creation! In Genesis 2:7, God formed man out of dust and then blew the breath of life into his nostrils so that he became a living being. At the Chrism Mass, which is celebrated by the bishop before Easter, he breathes over the three different vessels of oil that will be used for the sacraments. This gesture recalls Jesus' action in today's Gospel: a symbol of the Holy Spirit coming down to consecrate the oil. The Holy Spirit that is breathed into Adam, breathed over the sacred oils, and breathed onto the apostles gives life. The Holy Spirit is God's very life and it is within you also. At your baptism you received the gift of the Holy Spirit so that you can live your life for God as the apostles did after receiving the Holy Spirit at Pentecost.

......ON THE WAY TO MASS

Listen for the words Jesus says in today's Gospel: "Peace be with you." Where else in the Mass do we hear these words? Why do we say them?

ON THE WAY HOME FROM MASS ......

What do you think the disciples felt before Jesus came and stood in their midst? After he breathed on them, how do you think they felt?

Living the Word

The Holy Spirit is waiting to be invited into everything you do. As a family, make it a habit to invite him into your every activity by saying, "Come, Holy Spirit. You are welcome here." Invite him before driving, before school activities, or before a difficult conversation. He is waiting to be let in.

June 4, 2023

Solemnity of the Most Holy Trinity

Hearing the Word

John 3:16–18

In the name of the Father, and of the Son, and of the Holy Spirit.

God so loved the world that he gave his only Son, so that everyone who believes in him might not perish but might have eternal life. For God did not send his Son into the world to condemn the world, but that the world might be saved through him. Whoever believes in him will not be condemned, but whoever does not believe has already been condemned, because he has not believed in the name of the only Son of God.

Reflecting on the Word

The first verse of today's Gospel is one of the most popular verses in the whole Bible—and for good reason. In one line John is able to express the lengths to which God shows how much he loves us and wants us with him. God gave his Son, knowing that he would be misunderstood, an outcast, poor, and then painfully crucified like a criminal. Why would a father allow this? For love. He knew his love would not only save his Son but also us. God does not force us to love him back. We have a choice. We have a choice to believe and follow him so that we may have the eternal life that Jesus gave his life for: eternal love from an eternal King.

......ON THE WAY TO MASS

Why did God send us his son? Do you think it was hard for him to do?

ON THE WAY HOME FROM MASS ......

How does it make you feel knowing that God gave his only Son so that you can live for eternity with him?

Living the Word

John 3:16 is a popular verse of the Bible to memorize. As a family, memorize it together and see who knows it best by the end of the week! Ask your children why this verse is important for us to keep in our hearts.

June 11, 2023

Solemnity of the Most Holy Body and Blood of Christ

Hearing the Word

John 6:51–58

In the name of the Father, and of the Son, and of the Holy Spirit.

Jesus said to the Jewish crowds: "I am the living bread that came down from heaven; whoever eats this bread will live forever; and the bread that I will give is my flesh for the life of the world."

The Jews quarreled among themselves, saying, "How can this man give us his flesh to eat?" Jesus said to them, "Amen, amen, I say to you, unless you eat the flesh of the Son of Man and drink his blood, you do not have life within you. Whoever eats my flesh and drinks my blood has eternal life, and I will raise him on the last day. For my flesh is true food, and my blood is true drink. Whoever eats my flesh and drinks my blood remains in me and I in him. Just as the living Father sent me and I have life because of the Father, so also the one who feeds on me will have life because of me. This is the bread that came down from heaven. Unlike your ancestors who ate and still died, whoever eats this bread will live forever."

Reflecting on the Word

As Catholics, we believe that the eucharistic elements of bread and wine actually are Christ's Body and Blood. In today's Gospel, Jesus is speaking very directly about this. He does not say that the bread that he will give is *like* his flesh but that it *is* his flesh. Even when the Jews questioned him about giving his own flesh to eat (notice that even the Jews were taking him literally), Jesus answered, "unless you eat the flesh of the Son of Man and drink his blood, you do not have life within you." Why would Jesus want us to eat his flesh and drink his blood? Because in the same way that earthly bread nourishes our bodies, the Eucharist, the Bread of Life, the Body of Jesus Christ himself, nourishes our souls so that he can be with us in a very special way. He loves us that much!

......ON THE WAY TO MASS

For those children who have already had their First Holy Communion, ask them their memories about it. For the younger children who have not yet had their First Holy Communion, ask what they look forward to.

ON THE WAY HOME FROM MASS ......

What do you think Jesus meant by saying, "I am the living bread"?

Living the Word

Blessed Imelda Lambertini was a child who was devoted to the Eucharist. Research her story online and discuss it together.

June 18, 2023

Eleventh Sunday in Ordinary Time

Hearing the Word

Matthew 10:5–8

In the name of the Father, and of the Son, and of the Holy Spirit.

Jesus sent out the twelve after instructing them thus, "Do not go into pagan territory or enter a Samaritan town. Go rather to the lost sheep of the house of Israel. As you go, make this proclamation: 'The kingdom of heaven is at hand.' Cure the sick, raise the dead, cleanse lepers, drive out demons. Without cost you have received; without cost you are to give."

Reflecting on the Word

"Without cost you have received; without cost you are to give." Imagine if we lived every day like some children at Christmas, consumed only with receiving presents. The value of the gift depreciates, and we might take the people who gave us those gifts for granted. Yet if we spend time with each gift, understanding the value of it and growing in appreciation and gratitude, we are changed. Every day, God has an abundance of gifts for us that he gives freely. In today's Gospel, Jesus is asking us to be aware of what we have received from him without cost and asks for us to be generous with those around us in the same way.

•••••• ON THE WAY TO MASS

What are some gifts that you receive daily from God?

ON THE WAY HOME FROM MASS ••••••

How can you give without cost the same way you have received without cost?

Living the Word

Building a habit of gratitude opens your eyes to all the gifts that daily surround you and helps you see the world in a more positive light. Every day this week, have each member of your family name what they are thankful for that day. Ask them to share during a meal, or when everyone is in the car, or right before bedtime.

June 25, 2023

Twelfth Sunday in Ordinary Time

Hearing the Word

Matthew 10:26–33

In the name of the Father, and of the Son, and of the Holy Spirit.

Jesus said to the Twelve: "Do not be afraid. Nothing is concealed that will not be revealed, nor secret that will not be known. What I say to you in the darkness, speak in the light; what you hear whispered, proclaim on the housetops. And do not be afraid of those who kill the body but cannot kill the soul; rather, be afraid of the one who can destroy both soul and body in Gehenna. Are not two sparrows sold for a small coin? Yet not one of them falls to the ground without your Father's knowledge. Even all the hairs of your head are counted. So do not be afraid; you are worth more than many sparrows. Everyone who acknowledges me before others I will acknowledge before my heavenly Father. But whoever denies me before others, I will deny before my heavenly Father."

Reflecting on the Word

Do you know how many hairs are on your head? God does—he knows you better than you know yourself. There is nothing that you can hide from him, and you don't need to hide because God knows all of you and he still loves you. Sometimes there are things about ourselves that we are afraid to have others know, afraid they might not like us anymore or think badly of us. Our actions or choices don't change how God feels about each of us, his beloved son or daughter. How does that make you feel?

......ON THE WAY TO MASS

What does it say about God that he knows all secrets and even all the hairs on your head?

ON THE WAY HOME FROM MASS ......

If God knows everything about you, even how many hairs are on your head, what does that tell you about what he feels for you?

Living the Word

"Even all the hairs of your head are counted. So do not be afraid; you are worth more than many sparrows." Have your children copy this Scripture passage on paper and then draw a picture of themselves. Ask your children to draw strands of hair and count them together. Try counting each strand of hair on their heads. Can you finish counting? Talk about how God our loving Father already knows how many actual hairs on our head we have. What does that say about how intimately he knows us?

July 2, 2023

Thirteenth Sunday in Ordinary Time

Hearing the Word

Matthew 10:37–42

In the name of the Father, and of the Son, and of the Holy Spirit.

Jesus said to his apostles: "Whoever loves father or mother more than me is not worthy of me, and whoever loves son or daughter more than me is not worthy of me; and whoever does not take up his cross and follow after me is not worthy of me. Whoever finds his life will lose it, and whoever loses his life for my sake will find it.

"Whoever receives you receives me, and whoever receives me receives the one who sent me. Whoever receives a prophet because he is a prophet will receive a prophet's reward, and whoever receives a righteous man because he is righteous will receive a righteous man's reward. And whoever gives only a cup of cold water to one of these little ones to drink because he is a disciple—amen, I say to you, he will surely not lose his reward."

Reflecting on the Word

At first glance, today's Gospel seems harsh. Does Jesus not want us to love our fathers and mothers, or sons and daughters? Of course, he does! Many times in the Gospel accounts, he speaks about loving and obeying them. In this passage, however, Jesus is speaking about whom we love most. Jesus wants us to love him the most. Not because he is selfish but because he knows that when we love him first, we are better people. We are happier, we are more peaceful, we are fair and more respectful of others. When we put Jesus first in everything in our lives, everything else falls into place.

......ON THE WAY TO MASS

Jesus is asking us to love him before everything else. What are ways we can we do that every day?

ON THE WAY HOME FROM MASS ......

Jesus asks us to "take up our cross and follow him." What are some crosses in our lives? How can we follow Jesus with these crosses?

Living the Word

Have your family make a list of people and things that they love. When finished have everyone write *God* in large letters at the top of the list. How does loving God first help us to love everyone and everything else on the lists?

July 9, 2023

Fourteenth Sunday in Ordinary Time

Hearing the Word

Matthew 11:25–30

In the name of the Father, and of the Son, and of the Holy Spirit.

At that time Jesus exclaimed: "I give praise to you, Father, Lord of heaven and earth, for although you have hidden these things from the wise and the learned you have revealed them to little ones. Yes, Father, such has been your gracious will. All things have been handed over to me by my Father. No one knows the Son except the Father, and no one knows the Father except the Son and anyone to whom the Son wishes to reveal him.

"Come to me, all you who labor and are burdened, and I will give you rest. Take my yoke upon you and learn from me, for I am meek and humble of heart; and you will find rest for yourselves. For my yoke is easy, and my burden light."

Reflecting on the Word

"For although you have hidden these things from the wise and the learned you have revealed them to little ones." The smallest children have a capacity to understand God, far better than adults. They fully accept that God loves them—a notion that we start to lose as adults. Children do not need all the details; they are content with knowing that God loves them and wants to be with them. Children can reveal to us some of the deepest truths that God has "hidden" in the Scriptures. We have to be willing to listen. In another Scripture passage, Jesus encourages us to become like little children in order to enter the Kingdom of heaven. Children can show adults the path to God, rather than the other way around.

• • • • • • ON THE WAY TO MASS

Jesus has always chosen the small, the young, the poor, and little. Why do you think Jesus prefers these?

ON THE WAY HOME FROM MASS • • • • • •

I wonder what "hidden things" Jesus was speaking about that the "little ones" know.

Living the Word

This week read Matthew 18:1–5 as a family. Discuss what Jesus is revealing in this Scripture passage and how we should respond to it.

July 16, 2023

Fifteenth Sunday in Ordinary Time

Hearing the Word

Matthew 13:10–13

In the name of the Father, and of the Son, and of the Holy Spirit.

The disciples approached [Jesus] and said, "Why do you speak to them in parables?" He said to them in reply, "Because knowledge of the mysteries of the kingdom of heaven has been granted to you, but to them it has not been granted. To anyone who has, more will be given and he will grow rich; from anyone who has not, even what he has will be taken away. This is why I speak to them in parables, because *they look but do not see and hear but do not listen or understand.*"

Reflecting on the Word

Throughout the New Testament, Jesus talked about the Kingdom of heaven through the use of parables. With this method of teaching, he used something from everyday life—a seed, a woman making bread, a pearl, a shepherd—and revealed truths about himself or the Kingdom of heaven. When we ponder the truths in the parables and pray with them, something different might be revealed to us each time. For two thousand years, we have been pondering these parables and Jesus is still speaking to us through them.

· · · · · · ON THE WAY TO MASS

Why do you think Jesus taught in parables?

ON THE WAY HOME FROM MASS · · · · · ·

Parables are stories that teach a lesson. What lessons do you think Jesus wanted us to learn?

Living the Word

Some parables that are good for all ages are the parable of the mustard seed (Mark 4:30–32), the parable of the precious pearl (Matthew 13:45–46), and the parable of the found sheep (Luke 15:4–6). On different days this week, choose a parable to read and think about together. What is Jesus trying to reveal in this parable?

Sixteenth Sunday in Ordinary Time

Hearing the Word

Matthew 13:31–33

In the name of the Father, and of the Son, and of the Holy Spirit.

[Jesus] proposed another parable to them. "The kingdom of heaven is like a mustard seed that a person took and sowed in a field. It is the smallest of all the seeds, yet when full-grown it is the largest of plants. It becomes a large bush, and the 'birds of the sky come and dwell in its branches.'"

He spoke to them another parable. "The kingdom of heaven is like yeast that a woman took and mixed with three measures of wheat flour until the whole batch was leavened."

Reflecting on the Word

The Kingdom of heaven is so grand and mysterious that Jesus gives us these parables to help us ponder its greatness. We hear that the smallest of all seeds grows into the largest of plants, and the tiny yeast transforms flour into a large loaf of bread. Today's Gospel invites us to think deeply about how something so small can become something very large. It is our job now to take these images that Jesus gave us and use them as springboards to ponder the whole universe: history, nature, ourselves, and, of course, the Kingdom of heaven. What power made the mustard seed grow into the largest plant? We can see this power everywhere, this beautiful force that propels less to more.

......ON THE WAY TO MASS

Where in your life and throughout the universe do you see a growth of less to more?

ON THE WAY HOME FROM MASS ......

What happened to the mustard seed? What happens to bread when you add yeast? How is this like the Kingdom of heaven?

Living the Word

The parable of the growing seed (Mark 4:26–29) is very similar to the two in today's Gospel. This week read it together as a family and discuss how it is similar and different.

July 30, 2023

Seventeenth Sunday in Ordinary Time

Hearing the Word

Matthew 13:44–52

In the name of the Father, and of the Son, and of the Holy Spirit.

Jesus said to his disciples: "The kingdom of heaven is like a treasure buried in a field, which a person finds and hides again, and out of joy goes and sells all that he has and buys that field. Again, the kingdom of heaven is like a merchant searching for fine pearls. When he finds a pearl of great price, he goes and sells all that he has and buys it. Again, the kingdom of heaven is like a net thrown into the sea, which collects fish of every kind. When it is full they haul it ashore and sit down to put what is good into buckets. What is bad they throw away. Thus it will be at the end of the age. The angels will go out and separate the wicked from the righteous and throw them into the fiery furnace, where there will be wailing and grinding of teeth.

"Do you understand all these things?" They answered, "Yes." And he replied, "Then every scribe who has been instructed in the kingdom of heaven is like the head of a household who brings from his storeroom both the new and the old."

Reflecting on the Word

Jesus shares beautiful parables to help us ponder the grandness of the Kingdom of heaven. Today's parables reveal a different quality of God's Kingdom. A treasure buried in a field is so wonderful that, once discovered, brings much joy and changes the finder's whole life. A pearl that is so valuable that, once found, is worth all to the finder. Jesus told us these parables because he wants us to discover for ourselves how the Kingdom of heaven is like this treasure and pearl.

. . . . . . ON THE WAY TO MASS

Describe the Kingdom of heaven in one or two of your own words.

ON THE WAY HOME FROM MASS . . . . . .

Jesus compared the Kingdom of heaven to treasure, fine pearls, a great catch of fish that will be sorted, and an inventory of old and new items. Think about the words you used to describe the Kingdom of heaven. Are they similar or different from the Jesus' descriptions?

Living the Word

Read these five short parables about the Kingdom of heaven and discuss as a family what each is teaching us: Mark 4:30–32, Matthew 13:45–46, Matthew 13:33, Matthew 13:44, and Mark 4:26–29. What is similar between them, what is different? Remember there are no wrong answers.

August 6, 2023

Feast of the Transfiguration of the Lord

Hearing the Word

Matthew 17:1–8

In the name of the Father, and of the Son, and of the Holy Spirit.

Jesus took Peter, James, and John his brother, and led them up a high mountain by themselves. And he was transfigured before them; his face shone like the sun and his clothes became white as light. And behold, Moses and Elijah appeared to them, conversing with him. Then Peter said to Jesus in reply, "Lord, it is good that we are here. If you wish, I will make three tents here, one for you, one for Moses, and one for Elijah." While he was still speaking, behold, a bright cloud cast a shadow over them, then from the cloud came a voice that said, "This is my beloved Son, with whom I am well pleased; listen to him." When the disciples heard this, they fell prostrate and were very much afraid. But Jesus came and touched them, saying, "Rise, and do not be afraid." And when the disciples raised their eyes, they saw no one else but Jesus alone.

Reflecting on the Word

In today's Gospel, we hear God's voice: "This is my beloved Son, with whom I am well pleased; listen to him." Pope Francis said that "the first duty of the Christian is to listen to the Word of God, to listen to Jesus, because he speaks to us and saves us by his word" (Homily for Second Sunday of Lent, 2014). What do we spend our days listening to? It is so easy to listen to music, movies, news, or gossip, but how much time do we spend listening to Jesus by reading the Gospel accounts? In order to really listen to someone we must be willing to spend time with them, to learn about who they are so that we can better understand what they want to tell us. Are we willing to do that with Jesus?

......ON THE WAY TO MASS

What are some other ways that you can "listen to Jesus" more in your daily life?

ON THE WAY HOME FROM MASS ......

Pretend that you were there on the mountain with the apostles and Jesus. Talk about your experience. Did it help you know Jesus more, or not?

Living the Word

Forming good habits requires repetition. Every day this week as a family, try to read from the Gospel accounts. It does not have to be a long passage. Afterward, discuss what this passage reveals about who Jesus is.

August 13, 2023

Nineteenth Sunday in Ordinary Time

Hearing the Word

Matthew 14:26–33

In the name of the Father, and of the Son, and of the Holy Spirit.

When the disciples saw [Jesus] walking on the sea they were terrified. "It is a ghost," they said, and they cried out in fear. At once Jesus spoke to them, "Take courage, it is I; do not be afraid." Peter said to him in reply, "Lord, if it is you, command me to come to you on the water." He said, "Come." Peter got out of the boat and began to walk on the water toward Jesus. But when he saw how strong the wind was he became frightened; and, beginning to sink, he cried out, "Lord, save me!" Immediately Jesus stretched out his hand and caught Peter, and said to him, "O you of little faith, why did you doubt?" After they got into the boat, the wind died down. Those who were in the boat did him homage, saying, "Truly, you are the Son of God."

Reflecting on the Word

In the Gospel accounts, we have learned that Jesus has the power to heal sickness, command evil spirits, and even bring people back from the dead. In today's Gospel, we see that Jesus has power even over nature. Our creator God naturally has dominion over what he has made. Jesus walking on water is something that is not scientifically possible but we know that nothing is impossible for God.

······ ON THE WAY TO MASS

Name some other instances in the Bible in which God does the impossible.

ON THE WAY HOME FROM MASS ······

How do you think Peter felt when he first started walking on water toward Jesus? What made Peter start sinking? Whenever you feel afraid or doubtful, what do you do to help ease those fears or doubts?

Living the Word

Have everyone in the family draw a picture of one moment in today's Gospel story so that when the pictures are placed side by side, they tell the whole story. Tape them on the wall so that everyone remembers the Gospel this week.

August 15, 2023

Solemnity of the Assumption of the Blessed Virgin Mary

Hearing the Word

Luke 1:39–45

In the name of the Father, and of the Son, and of the Holy Spirit.

During those days Mary set out and traveled to the hill country in haste to a town of Judah, where she entered the house of Zechariah and greeted Elizabeth. When Elizabeth heard Mary's greeting, the infant leaped in her womb, and Elizabeth, filled with the Holy Spirit, cried out in a loud voice and said, "Most blessed are you among women, and blessed is the fruit of your womb. And how does this happen to me, that the mother of my Lord should come to me? For at the moment the sound of your greeting reached my ears, the infant in my womb leaped for joy. Blessed are you who believed that what was spoken to you by the Lord would be fulfilled."

Reflecting on the Word

Today's solemnity celebrates that Mary was taken into heaven body and soul. Her unique place in salvation history, her unique relationship with Jesus, and her unique soul without any stain of sin is why she receives this gift at the end of her life. In today's Gospel, we hear Elizabeth say to Mary that she is most blessed among women and blessed because she believed that what the Lord said to her would happen. Mary's faith allowed her to be open to God's will for her life, and through her, God brought salvation to all human life. Mary did not do any of this through her own ability but rather became an instrument of God's will. Mary is an example to us to have faith in God and to be open to his will for our lives so that he can do great things through us.

•••••• ON THE WAY TO MASS

When you think of Mary, what words come to mind to describe her?

ON THE WAY HOME FROM MASS ••••••

I wonder why Elizabeth's baby leaped in her womb when he heard Mary's greeting.

Living the Word

Elizabeth's words, "blessed are you among women, and blessed is the fruit of your womb," are used in the Hail Mary. As a family, pray a decade (ten Hail Marys) of the Rosary while thinking about today's Scripture, which is also the second Joyful Mystery.

Twentieth Sunday in Ordinary Time

Hearing the Word

Matthew 15:21–28

In the name of the Father, and of the Son, and of the Holy Spirit.

At that time, Jesus withdrew to the region of Tyre and Sidon. And behold, a Canaanite woman of that district came and called out, "Have pity on me, Lord, Son of David! My daughter is tormented by a demon." But Jesus did not say a word in answer to her. His disciples came and asked him, "Send her away, for she keeps calling out after us." He said in reply, "I was sent only to the lost sheep of the house of Israel." But the woman came and did Jesus homage, saying, "Lord, help me." He said in reply, "It is not right to take the food of the children and throw it to the dogs." She said, "Please, Lord, for even the dogs eat the scraps that fall from the table of their masters." Then Jesus said to her in reply, "O woman, great is your faith! Let it be done for you as you wish." And the woman's daughter was healed from that hour.

Reflecting on the Word

Did you know that almost everything we say in the Mass is from the Bible? When we know the stories behind the words we say, what we profess has so much more meaning. In today's Gospel, we hear a woman say to Jesus, "Have pity on me, Lord," or said in another way, "Have mercy on me, Lord." We say these powerful words at Mass when we are asking God to forgive us. In this moment we are repeating the Canaanite woman's plea for help. She had so much faith that even the "scraps" of his power were enough for her. Jesus knew that her faith would be an example to his own disciples! May she also be an example to us!

......ON THE WAY TO MASS

Pay attention to the Penitential Act at the beginning of Mass. Why is it important to ask for God's mercy and forgiveness at the start of the Mass?

ON THE WAY HOME FROM MASS ......

Jesus says that the Canaanite woman has great faith. How does she show great faith? How can we have faith like she does?

Living the Word

The words "Lord, have mercy" are sometimes repeated or sung in Greek, which is the original language of the Gospel accounts. As a family, explore the different ways this prayer can be said or sung:

Greek: *Kyrie eleison. Christe eleison. Kyrie eleison.*

English: Lord, have mercy. Christ, have mercy. Lord, have mercy.

Discuss which way each person prefers and why.

August 27, 2023

Twenty-First Sunday in Ordinary Time

Hearing the Word

Matthew 16:15–18

In the name of the Father, and of the Son, and of the Holy Spirit.

[Jesus said to his disciples:] "But who do you say that I am?" Simon Peter said in reply, "You are the Messiah, the Son of the living God." Jesus said to him in reply, "Blessed are you, Simon son of Jonah. For flesh and blood has not revealed this to you, but my heavenly Father. And so I say to you, you are Peter, and upon this rock I will build my church, and the gates of the netherworld shall not prevail against it."

Reflecting on the Word

Today, we hear Jesus ask the ultimate question: Who do you say that I am? He asked his disciples, and he is asking us as well. He wants to know who *you* say that he is. Not your priest, not your parents, not your friends, but you. Your authentic response can change your life. Peter doubted while walking on water, he denied Jesus in his time of need, and he was not educated in the temple. But notice that his response to who he believed Jesus was, what he truly believed in his heart about him, led Jesus to choose him to be the head of the Church. I wonder what Jesus could do with your answer.

• • • • • • ON THE WAY TO MASS

How would you answer Jesus' question: Who do you say that I am?

ON THE WAY HOME FROM MASS • • • • • •

I wonder how Simon Peter felt when Jesus said, "Blessed are you. . . . Upon this rock I will build my church." I wonder if he fully understood what Jesus was asking of him.

Living the Word

It is hard to answer Jesus' question with just one word. Simon Peter even had two different names for Jesus in his answer in today's Gospel. Write down everyone's answer to the question "Who do you say that Jesus is?" Look at the variety of ways Jesus reveals himself to us.

September 3, 2023

Twenty-Second Sunday in Ordinary Time

Hearing the Word

Matthew 16:21–25

In the name of the Father, and of the Son, and of the Holy Spirit.

Jesus began to show his disciples that he must go to Jerusalem and suffer greatly from the elders, the chief priests, and the scribes, and be killed and on the third day be raised. Then Peter took Jesus aside and began to rebuke him, "God forbid, Lord! No such thing shall ever happen to you." He turned and said to Peter, "Get behind me, Satan! You are an obstacle to me. You are thinking not as God does, but as human beings do."

Then Jesus said to his disciples, "Whoever wishes to come after me must deny himself, take up his cross, and follow me. For whoever wishes to save his life will lose it, but whoever loses his life for my sake will find it."

Reflecting on the Word

Jesus never said following him was going to be easy. He said he is the only source of complete joy, he will give us eternal life in heaven, but he never promises that our lives would have no burdens. Jesus tells us we must "take up our cross and follow him." Follow him where? Well, where did he go? To be crucified. But the story doesn't end on Good Friday. We follow him all the way to Easter Sunday. Jesus promises that his light will always be stronger than the darkness. But to get to that light, we must follow him.

......ON THE WAY TO MASS

What does it mean to follow Jesus?

ON THE WAY HOME FROM MASS ......

Do we ever act like Peter and stand as an obstacle for others on their journey to follow Jesus?

Living the Word

As a family, think of some people in your life who are good examples of following Jesus. Discuss how their lives have shown you how to follow Jesus, too.

EVERYDAY FAMILY PRAYERS

The Sign of the Cross

The Sign of the Cross is the first prayer and the last—of each day, and of each Christian life. It is a prayer of the body as well as a prayer of words. When we are presented for baptism, the community traces this sign on our bodies for the first time. Parents may trace it daily on their children. We learn to trace it daily on ourselves and on those whom we love. When we die, our loved ones will trace this holy sign on us for the last time.

In the name of the Father,

and of the Son,

and of the Holy Spirit. Amen.

The Lord's Prayer

The Lord's Prayer, or the Our Father, is a very important prayer for Christians because Jesus himself taught it to his disciples, who taught it to his Church. Today, we say this prayer as part of Mass, in the Rosary, and in personal prayer. There are seven petitions in the Lord's Prayer. The first three ask for God to be glorified and praised, and the next four ask for God to help take care of our physical and spiritual needs.

Our Father, who art in heaven,

hallowed be thy name;

thy kingdom come,

thy will be done

on earth as it is in heaven.

Give us this day our daily bread,

and forgive us our trespasses,

as we forgive those who trespass against us;

and lead us not into temptation, but deliver us from evil.

The Apostles' Creed

The Apostles' Creed is one of the earliest creeds we have; scholars believe it was written in the second century. The Apostles' Creed is shorter than the Nicene Creed, but it states what we believe about the Father, Son, and Holy Spirit. This prayer is sometimes used at Mass, especially at Masses with children, and is part of the Rosary.

I believe in God,

the Father almighty,

Creator of heaven and earth,

and in Jesus Christ, his only Son, our Lord,

who was conceived by the Holy Spirit,

born of the Virgin Mary,

suffered under Pontius Pilate,

was crucified, died and was buried;

he descended into hell;

and on the third day he rose again from the dead;

he ascended into heaven,

and is seated at the right hand of God the Father almighty;

from there he will come to judge the living and the dead.

I believe in the Holy Spirit,

the holy catholic Church,

the communion of saints,

the forgiveness of sins,

the resurrection of the body,

and life everlasting. Amen.

The Nicene Creed

The Nicene Creed was written at the Council of Nicaea in AD 325, when bishops of the Church gathered together in order to articulate true belief in who Christ is and in his relationship to God the Father. The Nicene Creed was the final document of that Council, written so that all the faithful may know the central teachings of Christianity. We say this prayer at Mass.

I believe in one God,

the Father almighty,

maker of heaven and earth,

of all things visible and invisible.

I believe in one Lord Jesus Christ,

the Only Begotten Son of God,

born of the Father before all ages.

God from God, Light from Light,

true God from true God,

begotten, not made, consubstantial with the Father;

through him all things were made.

For us men and for our salvation

he came down from heaven,

and by the Holy Spirit was incarnate of the Virgin Mary,

and became man.

For our sake he was crucified under Pontius Pilate,
he suffered death and was buried,
and rose again on the third day
in accordance with the Scriptures.
He ascended into heaven
and is seated at the right hand of the Father.
He will come again in glory
to judge the living and the dead
and his kingdom will have no end.

I believe in the Holy Spirit, the Lord, the giver of life,
who proceeds from the Father and the Son,
who with the Father and Son is adored and glorified,
who has spoken through the prophets.

I believe in one holy, catholic, and apostolic Church.
I confess one Baptism for the forgiveness of sins
and I look forward to the resurrection of the dead
and the life of the world to come. Amen.

Glory Be (Doxology)

This is a short prayer that Christians sometimes add to the end of psalms. It is prayed during the Rosary and usually follows the opening verse during the Liturgy of the Hours. It can be prayed at any time during the day.

Glory be to the Father

and to the Son

and to the Holy Spirit,

as it was in the beginning

is now, and ever shall be

world without end. Amen.

Hail Mary

The first two lines of this prayer are the words of the angel Gabriel to Mary, when he announces that she is with child (Luke 1:28). The second two lines are Elizabeth's greeting to Mary (Luke 1:42). The last four lines come to us from deep in history, from where and from whom we do not know. This prayer is part of the Rosary and is often used by Christians for personal prayer.

Hail, Mary, full of grace,

the Lord is with thee.

Blessed art thou among women

and blessed is the fruit of thy womb, Jesus.

Holy Mary, Mother of God,

pray for us sinners,

now and at the hour of our death.

Amen.

Grace before Meals

Families pray before meals in different ways. Some families make up a prayer in their own words, other families sing a prayer, and many families use this traditional formula. Teach your children to say this prayer while signing themselves with the cross.

Bless us, O Lord, and these thy gifts,

which we are about to receive from thy bounty,

through Christ our Lord.

Amen.

Grace after Meals

Teach your children to say this prayer after meals, while signing themselves with the cross. The part in brackets is optional.

We give thee thanks, for all thy benefits,

almighty God, who lives and reigns forever.

[And may the souls of the faithful departed,

through the mercy of God, rest in peace.]

Amen.

About the Author

Kerri Mecke-Lozano is a daughter of God, a wife, mother, missionary, and native Texan. She has been involved with Catechesis of the Good Shepherd since 2010. She is certified in Level I, II, and III, and is in the process of becoming a certified formation leader by CGSUSA. She has worked in atria in the United States and in Haiti. Kerri has a sociology degree from the University of Texas at San Antonio. She currently resides in central Texas with her husband, PJ, and their five children.